ATHLETICS IN THE ANCIENT WORLD

Classical World Series

Aristophanes and his Theatre of the Absurd, Paul Cartledge
Art and the Romans, Anne Haward
Athens and Sparta, S. Todd
Athens under the Tyrants, J. Smith
Attic Orators, Michael Edwards
Augustan Rome, Andrew Wallace-Hadrill
Cicero and the End of the Roman Republic, Thomas Wiedemann
Classical Archaeology in the Field, S.J. Hill, L. Bowkett and K. & D. Wardle
Classical Epic: Homer and Virgil, Richard Jenkyns
Democracy in Classical Athens, Christopher Carey
Environment and the Classical World, Patricia Jeskins
Greece and the Persians, John Sharwood Smith
Greek and Roman Historians, Timothy E. Duff
Greek and Roman Medicine, Helen King
Greek Architecture, R. Tomlinson
Greek Tragedy: An Introduction, Marion Baldock
Greek Vases Elizabeth Moignard
Julio-Claudian Emperors, T. Wiedemann
Lucretius and the Didactic Epic, Monica Gale
Morals and Values in Ancient Greece, John Ferguson
Mycenaean World, K. & D. Wardle
Plato's Republic and the Greek Enlightenment, Hugh Lawson-Tancred
Plays of Euripides, James Morwood
Plays of Sophocles, A.F. Garvie
Political Life in the City of Rome, J.R. Patterson
Religion and the Greeks, Robert Garland
Religion and the Romans, Ken Dowden
Roman Architecture, Martin Thorpe
Roman Britain, S.J. Hill and S. Ireland
Roman Satirists and Their Masks, Susanna Braund
Slavery in Classical Greece, N. Fisher
Women in Classical Athens, Sue Blundell

Classical World Series

ATHLETICS
IN THE
ANCIENT WORLD

Zahra Newby

Bristol Classical Press

First published in 2006 by
Bristol Classical Press
an imprint of
Gerald Duckworth & Co. Ltd.
90-93 Cowcross Street, London EC1M 6BF
Tel: 020 7490 7300
Fax: 020 7490 0080
inquiries@duckworth-publishers.co.uk
www.ducknet.co.uk

A catalogue record for this book is available
from the British Library

ISBN 1 85399 688 2
EAN 9781853996887

Typeset by Ray Davies

Contents

Acknowledgments

In writing this book I have been greatly helped by my experience of teaching university undergraduates about Greek athletics and festivals. In particular, I would like to thank all those Warwick students who chose to write their third-year dissertations on an aspect of ancient sport, and thus unwittingly allowed me to refine my own ideas. I am also very grateful to those who have provided images or allowed me to reproduce published material, and in particular to Brian Sparkes for allowing me to use his photograph of the Motya Youth. Thanks also go to my father, for reading the whole of the book and providing the perspective of the informed non-specialist, and to Andrew for technical help with maps and graphs. Deborah Blake at Duckworth has been a source of help and advice throughout. My warmest thanks go to all of them.

List of Figures and Sources

Notes on Spelling and Abbreviations

The decision on how to spell Greek words is always a difficult one. Here I have generally tried to use an exact transliteration of the Greek word (e.g. Patroklos rather than Patroclus) except where the Latinate spelling is so common in English that to use a transliteration would confuse (e.g. Achilles, gymnasium, stadium etc).

When referring to inscriptions I have also given references to source-books that are readily available, as below. With literary texts, I have only referred to sourcebooks for those that are otherwise difficult to find.

Arete = S.G. Miller, *Arete: Greek Sports from Ancient Sources* (Berkeley, Los Angeles and London, 3rd edn, 2004). Note that the numbering of sources differs in earlier editions.

Austin = M.M. Austin, *The Hellenistic World from Alexander to the Roman Conquest: A Selection of Ancient Sources in Translation* (Cambridge, numerous editions, most recently 1998).

IG = *Inscriptiones Graecae* (1873-)

PZenon = *Zenon papyri*

SEG = *Supplementum epigraphicum graecarum* (1923-)

Syll. = W. Dittenberger, *Sylloge Inscriptionum Graecarum*, 3rd edn (1915-24)

Other abbreviations follow the conventions of *The Oxford Classical Dictionary*, ed. S. Hornblower & A. Spawforth (3rd edn; Oxford, 1996).

Fig. 1. Map of Greece and Asia Minor
showing important places named in this book.

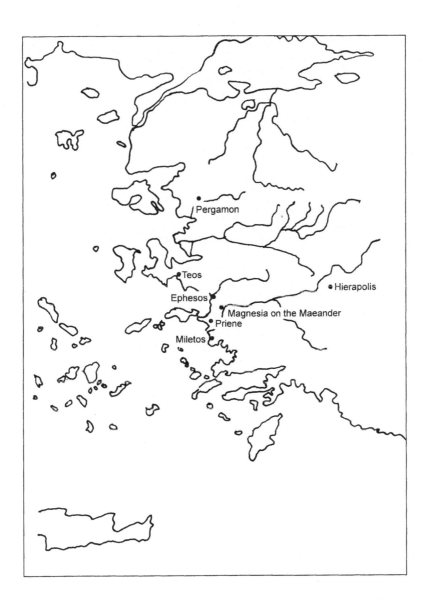

Chapter 1

Introduction: Modern Myths and Ancient Meanings

In modern life we are exposed to sport and athletics in a variety of forms. From the spectatorship of premier league football or the modern Olympic Games to personal training at the gym or involvement in team sports at school or university, we experience sport at a variety of different levels. There was a similar range of engagement in sport in the ancient world too, depending on whether one was competing in a public festival, training in the gymnasium, or watching others compete. Our understanding of ancient athletics is often influenced by our own experiences and attitudes, as well as by those of preceding generations. The way that a subject has been studied in the past also determines the sorts of questions that we address now, providing arguments and interpretations that modern scholars can either challenge or follow. I will start this enquiry into ancient sport by looking briefly at some of the ways in which research has been affected by more recent experiences.

In the study of ancient athletics inquiry has often concentrated on the ancient Olympic Games. In part, this is for very good reasons – in Antiquity too the Games at Olympia were understood as the prime example of an athletic festival (Philostratos, *Gymnastikos* 2). However, the revival of athletic games in the modern Olympics, instituted in 1896, can also cloud our understanding of ancient athletics. In particular, there is often a desire on the part of those holding the Games to create a direct link between themselves and the ancient world. This can encourage the belief that the modern Olympic Games are an accurate reflection of the ancient Games whereas in fact there are numerous differences. Some of the more obvious differences concern location and participation. In Antiquity the Games were always held in the same place, Olympia, whereas in modern times they move from city to city. The ancient Olympic Games were also restricted to Greek male citizens (though the definition of 'Greek' changed over time), with slaves and women banned from competing, and married women banned even from watching the Games on pain of death, with the exception of the priestess of Demeter (Pausanias 5.6.7; 6.20.9). Indeed, her presence reminds us of another major difference. In Antiquity the Games were part of a religious festival in honour of the god Zeus, part of a wider religious experience that included sacrifices and processions, as well as oaths sworn by the athletes to Zeus over slices of sacred boar's flesh (Pausanias 5.24.9).

In one area in particular the ideals of those who created the modern Games has profoundly affected our understanding of ancient athletics: the status of those who took part. When the modern Games were revived by the Frenchman Pierre de Coubertin in 1896 they were to be open only to amateur athletes, men of high social rank who did not need to earn money through their athletic pursuits. This amateur ideal profoundly affected a number of contemporary figures and has had a lasting effect on the scholarship of ancient athletics. One of the most important scholars of Greek athletics, E.N. Gardiner, firmly believed that the earliest Greek sportsmen were aristocratic amateurs who later gave way to lower-class professional athletes, in a development which he abhorred. This view can still be seen in a number of commonly-used textbooks, such as those of H.A. Harris, writing in the 1960s and 1970s. Yet recent scholars have convincingly challenged this view, showing that the concept of amateurism has no relevance in studies of the ancient world and that elite athletes continued to compete throughout the Greek and Roman periods. The social status of athletes is a subject tackled later in this book (Chapter 9), but it is important to note here that the ideological concerns of more recent figures can have a profoundly misleading effect on our view of the ancient past.

Another important area of confusion concerns the Olympic truce, or *ekecheiria*. This was a period of a month during which warfare by or against the Eleans (the city in charge of the sanctuary at Olympia) was forbidden in order to allow athletes safe passage to attend the games. Much has been made of this in modern times, and many commentators have pointed to the truce as a sign that the ancient Olympics spread peace and harmony among competing communities. In the words of the International Olympic Truce Foundation, a body that tries to use the modern Olympics as a means to promote peace among the nations of the world, 'Throughout the duration of the Olympic truce all conflicts ceased'. Yet this was far from the case. The truce prevented warfare only in the region of Elis and Olympia, rather than throughout the whole Greek world, and seems in some cases to have been ignored. We hear of an Athenian who was seized by Macedonian pirates in 348 BC despite the fact that it was the time of the Olympic truce (Aeschines, *On the Embassy* 12; cf. *Arete* 89). On another occasion, in 364 BC, there was even a pitched battle within the sanctuary while the Games were actually taking place, when Elis and her allies invaded to try to wrest control of the games back from their rivals Arcadia and Pisa (Xenophon, *Hellenica* 7.4.28-32).

Some ancient writers did associate the Games and their truce with attempts to promote inter-city concord and put a stop to civil strife (e.g. Pausanias 5.4.5), but their success would appear to have been limited. In modern times too, hopes of using the Games as a force for peace and understanding have often been undercut by political realities. During the Cold War the games were often used as an alternative battleground for the rivalry between East and West, and political boycotts occurred when the 1980 Games were held in Moscow and again in 1984 at Los Angeles. The power of politics to intrude into the sphere of sport was also horrifically revealed in the 1972 Munich Games when a group of Palestinian terrorists took hostage a number of the Israeli Olympic team in a siege which ultimately resulted in the deaths of all the hostages.

Politics have often lain behind struggles to hold the modern Games. One of the most vivid examples is the Berlin Olympics of 1936. These were used as a showcase to display the New Germany to the international community, with unrest strictly controlled. To commemorate the Games the brilliant filmmaker Leni Riefenstahl was commissioned to produce a film. The prologue to this clearly asserted the right of Nazi Germany to be seen as the heir to the ancient Greeks. Starting with misty shots of the ruins of Greece, it then showed the ancient past merging into the present as the ancient marble statue of Myron's discus-thrower melted into a shot of the German pentathlete Erwin Huber.

Ideological appropriations of the past, and of the associations of festivals and athletic activities, can be found in Antiquity too, particularly as Greek cities struggled to assert their individual identities in the Hellenistic and Roman periods. Yet while we sometimes find striking parallels between modern and ancient experiences of athletics, it is important also to be sensitive to the many differences between ancient and modern sport and athletics. These can be seen clearly in the words used to describe sporting activities. The Greek word for an athletic competition is *agon* – meaning contest – and the verb *athleuo* carries suggestions of struggle and competition as well as of physical activity. This is very different from the connotations of leisure and fun carried by the English words 'sport' and 'games'.

The rest of this book will show what we can learn about ancient Greek athletics from the eighth century BC through to the fourth century AD. Forms of sporting activity such as boxing and bull-leaping can be traced in earlier ancient societies too, especially in Minoan culture, as well as in Egyptian and near Eastern societies. Yet there seems to have been little direct influence of these cultures on later Greek history and I have no room to discuss them here. For reasons of space I have also omitted discussion of the sporting activities in Etruscan and early Roman culture. These seem primarily to have consisted of displays, often of boxing, put on by low-class or servile athletes for members of the upper classes to watch. Instead, this is a book about Greek athletics: the ways that it grew and developed throughout Greek history (including Greece's integration into the Roman Empire), and the functions that it served within society as a whole.

Chapter 2

Sources of Evidence

When enquiring into any aspect of the ancient world, there are a variety of different sources of evidence that we can draw upon, each with particular characteristics that must be taken into account. Broadly they fall into three main categories – literary evidence, evidence from inscriptions and archaeological evidence.

Literary evidence

This can include literary works specifically about athletics, as well as references to sport, festivals or the gymnasium that appear in other literary sources – whether in poetic, historical or philosophical works. Falling into the latter category are the references to athletic competitions that we find in the poems of Homer, discussed in the next chapter, or Thucydides' comments about the Greek practice of exercising naked. Works concentrating particularly on athletics include the victory odes of Pindar, composed to praise athletic victors at the Panhellenic festivals of Olympia, Delphi, Isthmia and Nemea.

A number of other works were written during the period of the Roman Empire. They include Lucian's comic dialogue (*Anacharsis*) between the Athenian law-giver Solon and a foreigner to Athens, the Scythian Anacharsis, over the usefulness of athletic training and competition, as well as Philostratos' treatise on athletic training, the *Gymnastikos*. With all these works it is important to consider first who the author is and why he is writing: clearly Pindar is aiming to praise and flatter his clients – he will present an idealised view of the associations of athletic victory, which is important in telling us about the virtues associated with sporting activity, but might not have been accepted by all. Writers from the Roman period also have their own agenda – they were writing in a period when Greece was eager to lay claim to her Classical past. Some of the practices which they present as direct survivals from that period, such as the notorious whipping ritual at Sparta (p. 88), can actually be shown by other evidence to be more recent inventions. They tell us about the importance for imperial

Greeks of creating a link with the past, but do not necessarily tell us the factual truth about what happened in that past.

Epigraphical evidence

Epigraphy is the study of inscriptions, texts inscribed into marble or bronze that were set up in public places around ancient cities. Inscriptions cover a multitude of subjects – laws decreed by the city, dedications made in sanctuaries, the honours voted to a particular benefactor or the buildings that such a benefactor had funded. They can give us a greater sense of day-to-day life than literary texts, but like texts they also serve individual desires and aspirations. Inscriptions that record gifts by a particular individual tell us how that individual wanted his city to see him – as a generous donor, or the pious worshipper of a particular god.

Inscriptions usually accompanied the statues of athletic victors that were set up in sanctuaries such as Olympia. While the precious bronze statues have usually been lost, melted down for the value of their material, their inscribed bases often survive. Indeed, at Olympia a number of inscribed bases were found in the excavations and can be put alongside the literary evidence provided by the traveller Pausanias, who described the sanctuary as it appeared during a visit in the second century AD. The inscriptions both support and modify Pausanias' account, showing that his description is based in reality, but also that he chooses statues from the Archaic and Classical periods over more recent ones (for a definition of these periods see pp. 96-7).

As with other sources of evidence, we have to be careful how we use inscriptions. Lists of athletic victors show us that the competitors who went to Olympia were gradually drawn from a larger and larger area (Chapter 4), but there might be particular factors skewing this evidence. Some areas seem to have used inscriptions in their civic life more than others did, while patterns of excavation and survival could result in particular areas being documented more heavily than others. This, of course, is one of the excitements of enquiry into the ancient world – at any point a new discovery might change our existing picture of how things really were.

A related form of evidence is provided by papyrus fragments, which have been found in great numbers in Egypt. One particular group of papyri contains the archive of a man called Zenon who lived during the second century BC. Among this correspondence is a series of letters relating to the education of a boy called Pyrrhos which include details about his training in athletics (e.g. *PZenon* 59060 = *Arete* 207).

Visual and archaeological evidence

We've already touched on the fact that many inscriptions originally accompanied bronze or marble statues. While many of these have been lost, occasionally the sea-bed yields finds such as the Riace bronzes, masterpieces of ancient bronze casting. Many more Greek statues can be visualised through the marble copies that were made of them in the Roman period, though we cannot always be sure which of these classicising works go back to particular Greek masterpieces. While we can often only speculate as to the original significance and location of these works, they help us to imagine the sorts of athletic statues that thronged ancient cities and sanctuaries (Chapter 7).

Other sorts of artistic evidence are also available to show us both the detail and the importance of ancient athletics. Athenian vases, in particular, often feature scenes of exercise in the gymnasium on cups and vessels used in the symposium (private dinner-and-drinking parties) while a particular set of vases, Panathenaic amphorae, were given as prizes to athletes in the Panathenaia festival at Athens. These show the patron goddess of the city, Athena, on one side, while the other is decorated with a scene of a specific contest, such as wrestling or boxing.

Artistic evidence can often illuminate obscure references in the literary sources, showing us the positions and techniques used for throwing the discus and javelin, or how jumping weights were used in the long jump (see Fig. 17). It gives us a sense of how the gymnasium fitted into civic life and its role as a place for male social and erotic activity (Chapter 11). Yet it too has limitations. Attic vases cannot be taken to describe the case in every Greek city, and artistic constraints (such as the shape of the space to decorate) may lie behind the choice of specific scenes. In one case, the so-called *perizoma* vases which were exported to Etruria in Italy, loincloths (*perizomata*) seem to have been deliberately added to figures of naked athletes to satisfy the cultural expectations of their Etruscan viewers. These vases have previously led to confusion about whether all Greek athletes did indeed exercise naked at the time these vases were produced, around 510 BC. The answer seems to be that they did, but that the loincloths were added to appease Etruscan moral sensitivities.

As well as artistic evidence such as vases, statues and other smaller objects such as figurines or gems, we can also learn about ancient athletics from the archaeological remains of athletic complexes. This fleshes out the picture by showing the stadia in which athletes competed as well as the gymnasia in which they trained. The appearance of gymnasia in diverse areas of the ancient world can also act as a sign of the diffusion of athletic training and Greek culture more generally across the Mediterranean world. When taken together, all these sources of evidence can help us to build up a detailed picture of how sport and athletics were practised and experienced in the ancient world.

Chapter 3

The Earliest Athletics: Games in Homer

Our earliest literary sources for Greek athletics can be found in the epic poems of Homer, the *Iliad* and the *Odyssey*. Much about Homer is uncertain – including his date, origin and to what extent one individual was responsible for the composition of these two famous poems – but those are matters to be debated elsewhere. We shall adopt here the general view that Homer was active around the middle of the eighth century BC and was composing his tales in a tradition of oral poetry, recalling events thought to have occurred some four and a half centuries earlier, towards the end of the Mycenaean period.

One important question when considering the treatment of athletic activity in the poems is whether we can use them in any sense as a historical source. Of course, they are primarily literature, and we have to look at how the scenes described fit into the overall plots of the poems. Yet it is reasonable to expect that Homer would not have included scenes that were obviously implausible to his audience. This raises another question – whether the scenes depicted refer to the ways sport was used during Homer's own lifetime, in the eighth century, or to eighth-century beliefs about athletics in the period of the Trojan War. The most likely answer is that it includes a little of both, but before we continue, let us look at what Homer actually says.

Athletic contests appear in both the *Iliad* and the *Odyssey*, but in rather different contexts. In *Iliad* 23 (257-897) they are held as part of the ceremonies associated with the burial of Achilles' companion Patroklos, as funeral games, while in the *Odyssey* they occur as part of the entertainment offered to Odysseus during his visit to the land of Phaiakia (*Odyssey* 8.97-255). The *Iliad*'s account is longer and more detailed. Achilles holds the contests as part of the honouring of his dead comrade and himself selects prizes for the contestants from his own, and Patroklos', possessions. All the Greek army are present and a number of famous warriors take part in the contests. These include the chariot race, which is described first and at length, then contests in boxing, wrestling, a foot race, armed combat, throwing a weight and in archery. A final contest in throwing a spear is forestalled when Achilles declares Agamemnon the winner before the contest even takes place. For all of these events Achilles sets out prizes, not just for the victor, but also for the other contestants. These are of high value and include vessels made of precious metals, such as bowls, cauldrons and tripods, as well as livestock and serving women. Weapons and armour are also given as prizes in the armed combat and archery contests.

The competitors include the most famous figures of the Greek army, such as Menelaos, Odysseus, Diomedes and the two Ajaxes, as well as lesser known figures such as the boxer Epeios who admits that he may not be as good at war, but states that he is pre-eminent in boxing (23.667-71). During the contests they are helped and hindered by the gods in much the same way as they are in battle. When Apollo robs Diomedes of his whip in the chariot race to favour his own protégé Eumelos, Athena angrily replaces it and wrecks the yoke of Eumelos' chariot for good measure, causing him to be thrown out of it. When Ajax slips in a pile of cow dung during the foot race, allowing Odysseus to win, this is also attributed to the will of Athena (23.774) – clearly a useful goddess to have on one's side! The same rivalries and concerns for honour that run throughout the poem can also be seen in these contests. Nestor offers advice to his son Antilokhos to take care to keep his horses as close as possible to the turning post without crashing into it, lest 'you bring injury upon your horses and chariot, delighting others and bringing shame upon yourself' (23.341-2). When Antilokhos manages to bypass Menelaos by some crafty daredevil overtaking, Menelaos reacts angrily, accusing him of deliberately fouling him, a situation that is only resolved when the younger man offers to give up his prize to Menelaos, who in turn refuses it, his honour satisfied.

If we analyse these events as part of the literary construction of the poem we can see the funeral games for Patroklos as a resolution of the tensions that have dogged the Achaian army up to this point. Achilles' generosity to the contestants and, in particular, the honour done Agamemnon (who is given the prize for spear-throwing without any contest taking place) shows that Achilles' separation from his fellow warriors is finally at an end. Athletics is also shown as an essential part of the Homeric warrior's lifestyle – when not fighting, these men spend their time competing in athletics instead. Here the games are in honour of a fallen comrade, and there are references to other funeral games too, such as those in which Nestor competed during his youth in honour of Amarykeus (23.631-2) and those for Oedipus (23.679).

In the *Odyssey*, by contrast, we find contests that are purely for entertainment and relaxation. These are the games that take place during

Odysseus' stay in Phaiakia as part of the hospitality offered by the king Alkinoos. After a long feast in which the guests are entertained by the bard Demodokos, the king suggests that they adjourn for some sport. The young noblemen of Phaiakia compete in a variety of contests – the foot race, wrestling, jumping, throwing the discus and boxing. The account is shorter than that in the *Iliad* and we do not hear of any prizes granted to the victors, probably because these contests take part primarily as a form of entertainment and leisure rather than in a formal competition. When Odysseus is invited to take part himself he rejects the idea, scornfully saying that he has better things on his mind (*Odyssey* 8.153-7). When one youth, Euryalos, suggests that this is because he is inferior, Odysseus is stung by the slight and jumps up to show that he can excel in all contests. He gets only as far as the discus throw, however, before the king's diplomacy intervenes by bringing on music and dancers. Here athletics appear to belong to the leisure time of the elite, but Odysseus' defence of his abilities links athletics with military training, mentioning his prowess in archery and throwing the javelin as well as in other contests.

There are both similarities and differences between these games and those that appear in the historical record for Archaic and Classical Greece. The prizes in *Iliad* 23 are particularly interesting. While each competitor strives for overall victory, the effort of all is rewarded with even the last place meriting a prize of some value. The dress of the athletes is also important. In the description of the boxing and wrestling, we hear that the athletes took off their tunics and put on loincloths, as well as binding their hands with thongs for the boxing match. The complete nudity that was such a conspicuous feature of later Greek athletics (see pp. 71-2),) is not present in Homer.

Some of the contests that occur here can be seen in later athletic festivals, but with some differences. Homer's heroes compete with the two-horse chariots used in battle, rather than in four-horse chariots, and they drive them themselves instead of using hired charioteers. The contests also seem to be especially related to war, as with the archery contest which we do not find in later festivals such as that at Olympia. The contests in throwing the spear and discus also appear here as separate events, rather than as part of the pentathlon as later. As mentioned above, it is very difficult to distinguish between features that might describe Homer's own day and those which relate to his picture of the past age of heroes. However, it seems likely that the picture combines elements of both, reflecting Homer's own experience of athletics as something that the aristocracy might take part in for leisure as well as during the celebrations marking the life and death of a prominent man. Indeed, a number of later festivals are said to have been first held as funeral games – such as those at Isthmia and Nemea for the babies Melikertes/Palaimon and Opheltes/Archemoros. Athletic pursuits also feature as part of the lifestyle of ancient heroes in Athenian tragedy in the fifth century BC. In particular, Sophokles' *Elektra* (680-763) includes a long account of a chariot race in which Orestes is (falsely) said to have perished. It is interesting that Homer does not include athletic contests among the honours offered to the gods – sacrifices are accompanied by the signing of hymns, but not by any forms of competition, unlike later Greek festivals. It is to the origins of such festivals, like the most famous athletic festival at Olympia, that we turn next.

Part I

Competitive Athletics and Festival Culture

Athletic activity in the ancient world falls into two main categories – competitive athletics in public religious festivals, where the victors won prizes and were honoured with statues or poems, and sporting activities as part of the leisure and education of male citizens, which took place primarily within the confines of the gymnasium. As we will see, the boundaries between these two worlds were flexible. The gymnasium served as the training ground for performance athletes and statues of famous victors could serve as role models for the youths in the gymnasium. However, in the majority of cases only a select few of those who exercised in the gymnasium would go on to compete and win in great events such as those at Olympia. In this section we will look at how those festivals developed and functioned, before turning in Part II to the roles played by athletics in education and leisure.

Chapter 4

The Games at Olympia

Throughout Antiquity the Games at Olympia provided the supreme model of a Panhellenic athletic festival. In his treatise on athletic training, the *Gymnastikos*, the third-century AD author Philostratos starts his discussion of the origins of different athletic contests by urging us to look at how things were done in Olympia, for these, he claims, are the most accurate sources (*Gymnastikos* 2). But how did the Games at Olympia come about, and what did they really mean?

According to tradition, the festival at Olympia began in 776 BC, at which point only one contest was included, the foot race. This was called the *stadion*, stade race, because the runners raced the length of the stadium (600 ancient feet – approximately 192 m at Olympia, though the length of stadia varies at different places). For most of Olympia's history, until the festival was finally abolished, probably at the end of the fourth century AD, the victor in the stade race had the honour of having that particular Olympic year named after him. The fact that the Greeks used Olympiads (the four-year period from one Olympic Games to the next) to date historical events just goes to show what an extensive influence this festival had over Greek life.

However, the ancient Greeks believed that the origins of the contests at Olympia lay beyond this traditional date, back in the mythical past, and that the 776 introduction was in fact a revival of an older contest instituted by gods or heroes. The writer Pausanias, who visited Olympia sometime between AD 160 and 180, gives a good idea of the many conflicting traditions which had been passed down by his time (Pausanias 5.7.6-5.8.4). One version gave the origins of the Games to the Cretan Kouretes, a set of five brothers appointed by the goddess Rhea to protect her infant son, Zeus. One of these, who was called Herakles (not the famous Herakles of the Twelve Labours), instituted running races between his brothers and crowned the victor with wild olive – the very plant that was used in later periods to form the victory wreath at Olympia. Others say that Zeus himself wrestled with his father Kronos here or instituted the Games to commemorate his victory over his father, whom he had ousted from his throne, and that the Olympian gods all took part.

According to other reports, the Games were particularly associated with Pelops who had won control of the region after defeating the previous king Oinomaos in a chariot race and winning the hand of his daughter Hippodameia. According to the myth, Oinomaos was accustomed to challenging his daughter's suitors to a chariot race, which he, being in possession of divine horses, always won. He then killed the unfortunate suitor and placed his head above the gates of his palace. When it came to the race with Pelops, however, some versions of the myth say that Oinomaos' charioteer Myrtilos was bribed to replace the pins securing the chariot wheels to the axle with ones made of wax, with the result that they melted and Oinomaos was thrown to his death. Another account, more favourable to Pelops, has him secure victory through the gift of a winged chariot from Poseidon (Pindar, *Olympian* 1.86-8). The importance of this event as a precursor for the Olympic Games can be seen in the fact that it was chosen to decorate the east pediment of the Temple of Zeus at Olympia, constructed *c.* 470-460 BC. Zeus stands in the centre, overseeing the preparations for the race, while Oinomaos and his wife stand on one side and Pelops and Hippodameia to the other (Fig. 2).

2. A reconstruction of the east façade of the Temple of Zeus at Olympia, showing the contest of Pelops and Oinomaos in the pediment.

Another popular contender for the origin of the games was the famous hero of the Twelve Labours, Herakles, whose labours took place in this area of southern Greece. In one of these he cleaned out the Augean stables by diverting the course of the local river Alpheios to flow through them. Herakles also features on the Temple of Zeus, in the metopes above the front and back of the temple, and Pindar, in particular, attributes the origins of the Games to a commemoration of this epic deed (Pindar, *Olympian* 10.24-54).

The ancient Greeks, then, clearly had a sense that the Olympic festival went back into the mists of time, and that their own contests here could be seen as a continuation of the activities of heroes and gods. But what about the reality? This too is somewhat elusive. Although the historical festival is closely associated with the worship of the god Zeus, some have suggested that the origins of cult and competition here should instead be associated with the worship of the hero Pelops. A monumental enclosure dedicated to the hero was set at the centre of the sanctuary, and was the site for the sacrifice to him of a black ram (Pausanias 5.13.1-2). Excavations in the sanctuary have yielded a number of dedications dating from *c.* 1000-750 BC, but especially from the eighth century BC, including representations of two-horse chariots and tripods. Given the importance of the chariot race in Homer, and the fact that tripods are there listed among the prizes awarded at the Games of Patroklos, many see these dedications as evidence of early athletic and chariot contests at Olympia, possibly deriving from funeral games in honour of the hero Pelops. However, more recent excavations have questioned the existence of an early cult to Pelops, arguing that the archaeological evidence only supports the presence of a cult to Pelops from the early fourth century BC. The literary tradition is also contradictory. According to the victor list composed by Hippias of Elis in around 400 BC, and later followed by Pausanias and Philostratos, the games traditionally began in 776 BC and at first included only one contest, a foot race the length of the stadium. According to this list, the chariot race was only introduced in 680 BC.

There are various ways in which we might try to reconcile the literary and archaeological evidence. Perhaps the dedications are simply offerings to the god, with no link to specific competitions (it is notable that they show two-horse chariots, rather than the four-horse ones recorded in the Olympic victory lists). We might also question the veracity of Hippias' account. One line of argument suggests that there was no early cult of Pelops here at all and the Games began, in honour of Zeus, around 700 BC, at precisely the time that archaeological evidence shows that wells were dug to provide water for the contestants. According to this view, the

Altis (as the sanctuary was known) was first and foremost a sanctuary to Zeus, with the Games being a secondary addition. The discrepancy between the traditional date of 776 and the archaeological date of c. 700 BC has also been explained by suggesting that the first games were held annually, and only later changed to a four-yearly cycle, but that Hippias erroneously assumed that they had always been held four-yearly and so backdated them to 776 BC.

Absolute certainty about the origins of the Games is impossible, and in many ways it is more interesting to look at what the Greeks of the later periods believed and why, than at how accurate those beliefs actually were. What can be said is that a sanctuary was present on the site from around 1000 BC and that it received increasing numbers of dedications in the eighth century, around the time that the Olympics were traditionally thought to have begun. Judging from the names recorded by Hippias and others, the initial contestants were mostly drawn from the Peloponnese (the first victor, Koroibos of Elis, coming from the city that maintained the sanctuary) and only in the sixth century did the Olympic Games come to be a truly Panhellenic festival, attracting contestants from the wider Greek world.

The contests

Leaving aside the matter of its accuracy, here is the traditional account of the order in which various contests were introduced to Olympia:

776 BC	*Stadion* race (the length of the stadium, approx 200 m)
724 BC	*Diaulos* race (two lengths of the stadium, approx 400 m)
720 BC	*Dolichos*, long race
708 BC	Wrestling (*pale*)
	Pentathlon – involving contests in the *stadion*, wrestling, the long jump (*halma*), throwing the discus and throwing the javelin (*akon*)
688 BC	Boxing (*pyx/pygme*)
680 BC	Four-horse chariot race (other equestrian races were introduced later too)
648 BC	*Pankration* – a combination of boxing and wrestling in which almost everything was allowed, with the exception of biting and gouging.
From 632 BC	Various boys' versions of the above contests introduced

As you will see from this list, the concentration was very firmly on individual events of the type now known as track and field events, divided into versions for both men and boys (other festivals sometimes included a third division, for beardless youths). Team contests such as ball games and rowing competitions did occasionally take place in the ancient world but usually formed part of the education and training of young citizens rather than being held as events at Panhellenic festivals.

There was also a distinction between athletic contests and equestrian ones. These included horse races and chariot-racing involving varying numbers of horses, mules and foals in addition to the four-horse chariot listed above. While these contests were keenly contested and brought great fame, they often involved hired jockeys or charioteers who rode horses or drove chariots belonging to members of the wealthy elites. The owner won the right of setting up a victory monument, while he or she may not have been directly involved in the competition itself. Indeed, this was one area where women could compete at the Olympic Games where they were otherwise excluded from both competition and spectatorship (with the exception of the priestess of Demeter and unmarried girls). One Spartan woman, Kyniska, the daughter of King Archidamos, proudly boasted on her victory monument that she alone of women had won the chariot race here (*Inschriften von Olympia* 160 = *Arete* 151b, *c*. 396 BC; cf. Pausanias 3.8.1). She was soon followed by others.

Development of the Games

It is likely that the earliest contests at Olympia were a purely local affair, attracting competitors from Elis and other neighbouring cities. Yet in time they came to be truly Panhellenic, attracting contestants from across the ancient world. Safe access to the Games in times of warfare was secured by the Olympic truce (see above, Chapter 1). It was believed that this had been introduced by Iphitos in 776 BC. It was inscribed on a discus known as the discus of Iphitos, which was kept in the Temple of Hera at Olympia (Pausanias 5.20.1). Other similar arrangements came into place to defend those attending the other Panhellenic festivals later instituted at Delphi, Isthmia and Nemea.

The fact that the Sanctuary at Olympia attracted worshippers and contestants from across the Greek world made it develop into an important centre of Greek identity and culture. For some, the fact that Greeks all came to worship at the same site was an argument in favour of Panhellenic unity, and against the frequent inter-city warfare and rivalry which was such a feature of Classical Greek history (Aristophanes, *Lysistrata* 1128-34). Yet in reality those rivalries were played out as much here as anywhere else. Numerous Greek states dedicated monuments in the Altis recording victories over their foes. Some of these celebrated victories over non-Greek enemies, such as a statue of Zeus that celebrated the victory of the Greeks over the Persians at Plataea in 479 BC and was inscribed with the names of all the cities that took part (Pausanias 5.23.1-3). Numerous others, however, commemorated victories over fellow Greek cities. Indeed, the very Temple of Zeus that dominated the centre of the Sanctuary was funded by the spoils of a war Elis had conducted against the rival city of Pisa (Pausanias 5.10.2). As we shall see, such fierce

3. The changing origins of Olympic Victors over time. The bar charts show the victors known from a particular area as a percentage of all the victors known for that period.

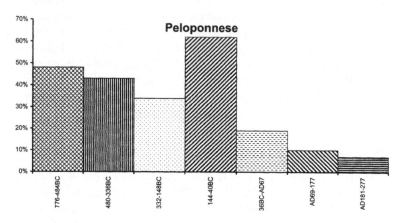

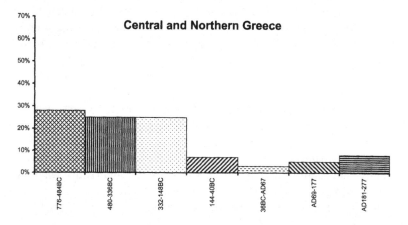

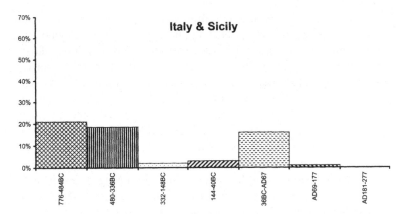

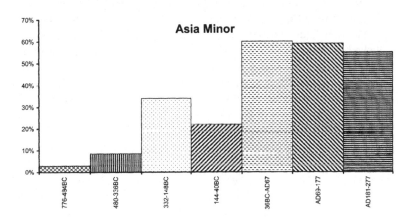

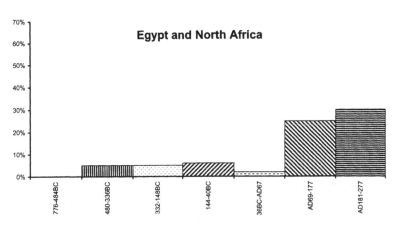

inter-city rivalries were also a prominent feature of the athletic contests.

From a variety of inscriptional and literary evidence we can trace the development of the Games and in particular the origins of those who were victorious here at various times. While our evidence is fragmentary and may be subject to certain biases (not least the changing preferences for setting up inscriptions recording such victories in different areas over time) nevertheless a clear picture does emerge (Fig. 3). According to this, victors at the games initially came from Greece itself, particularly from Elis and Sparta in the Peloponnese, and then from the Greek cities of Southern Italy and Sicily (Magna Grecia). As we proceed into the Hellenistic and Roman periods, however, victors from Magna Grecia and the Greek mainland decline in favour of increasing numbers from Asia Minor and, in the imperial period, Egypt and North Africa.

There are a number of explanations for this. One of the most convincing is to link it with the concept of Greek identity. It would seem that in the Archaic and Classical periods the cities of Magna Grecia particularly relished the opportunity the Olympic Games gave them to show their membership of the Greek world. After a general decline in the Late Republican period, during which the festival seems especially to have attracted local competitors (a third of those attested come from Elis itself), the increasing numbers of victors coming from Asia Minor and then Egypt probably reflects a similar aspiration to prove the Greekness of these areas. As they were gradually integrated into the Greek world following the conquests of Alexander the Great and the new city foundations of Hellenistic kings, Greek cities in the areas now occupied by modern Turkey, Syria, the Lebanon and Egypt eagerly took on the Greek culture of the gymnasium and could use the boast of having produced victors at the Olympic Games as support for their claims to Greek identity (cf. Austin 121). This may have been particularly important for those on the edges of the Greek world. In the fifth and fourth centuries BC too we see the Olympics used to prove tenuous claims to Greekness. One telling example is the struggle of the Macedonian kings to be accepted as members of the Greek race. According to Herodotos (5.22), when Alexander I of Macedon wished to compete at Olympia in the early fifth century BC he was initially turned down on the grounds that he was a foreigner. However, having argued his descent from the Argives he was allowed to enter the stadion race. Subsequent Macedonian kings also took part at Olympia, particularly in the equestrian contests, where in 356 BC Philip II won the horse race.

This broadening of the limits of participation does not mean that Olympic victories ceased to be important in mainland Greece. While we have fewer recorded victories for mainland Greece in the Olympics in the imperial period, Olympic victory still seems to have held an important ideological link to Greek identity. Statues of past victors continued to be cherished and revered, proving a city's claims to full membership of the Greek world.

Chapter 5

The Rise of a Festival Culture

The Olympic Games were not the only festival in Antiquity, though they were credited with being one of the most ancient. Indeed, the early sixth century BC saw the rise of the three other festivals which were later to form with the Olympics the festival circuit, or *periodos*: the Pythian Games in honour of Apollo at Delphi, dating from 586 BC, the Isthmian Games at the Isthmus of Corinth, in honour of Poseidon, instituted in 582 BC, and the Nemean Games in honour of Zeus, founded in 573 BC. Of these the Olympic and Pythian Games were held every four years (or in Greek terms, since they counted inclusively, every five years, leading to the title *penteric*) whereas the other two were held every two years. Victories at all four games led to the honour of being called a circuit-victor, *periodonikes*, a title that appears on numerous victory inscriptions. While the Olympic and Nemean Games included only athletic and equestrian events, those at Delphi and Isthmia also included musical contests. Indeed at Delphi these seem to have been dominant from the start, appropriately, given their context as part of the worship of the god Apollo who was closely associated with musical and poetic inspiration as the leader of the Muses. As at Olympia the prizes awarded in these games were simple wreaths of foliage – wild olive at Olympia, laurel at Delphi, pine at Isthmia and wild celery at Nemea. Apples are also mentioned as a prize at Delphi in later periods.

In addition to the development of the Panhellenic circuit, other games were also introduced as part of civic festivals. One of the most well-known examples is the Panathenaic Games at Athens, held in honour of the patron goddess Athena. Every four years an especially lavish version of the festival was celebrated as the great Panathenaia, with a full programme of athletic, equestrian and musical contests. This too was instituted in the early sixth century, in 566/5 BC. Yet there were differences between the four Panhellenic games and local festivals like the Panathenaia. The Panhellenic games were held at sanctuaries deemed to be open to all the Greeks, even if they were administered by particular Greek states, whereas the Panathenaia took place within the city-state of Athens, though like the Panhellenic festivals it and many other local festivals could attract competitors from across the Greek world. The prizes also differed. Although in their earliest days the contests at Olympia and Delphi may have awarded valuable prizes such as metal tripods, for the majority of their history the prizes were simple crowns of vegetation. These types of festivals are often referred to as 'crown' or 'sacred' games (*agones stephanitai* or *hieroi*). In contrast games such as those at Athens awarded monetary prizes. An inscription from the first half of the fourth century BC lists the prizes awarded in various contests (*IG* II 2311 = *Arete* 120). These included cash prizes for victories in the musical contests and containers full of valuable Attic olive oil (Panathenaic amphorae) for the athletic contests. Unlike at Olympia, where only the winner gained a crown, here prizes were also available for second place and occasionally even beyond. Festivals which gave cash prizes instead of simple crowns are often called *thematitai* or *chrematitai* after the Greek words for money and property.

Games in the Hellenistic period

As time went on more and more festivals were instituted around the Greek world. Much of our evidence for these comes from inscriptions – from the lists of victories set up by successful athletes, or from records of the diplomatic efforts involved in setting up the festivals. The Hellenistic period, in particular, marks the rise of a number of new festivals. A series of inscriptions record the efforts of Magnesia on the Maeander in western Asia Minor (modern-day Turkey) to set up a festival in honour of her patron goddess Artemis Leukophryene. They show that Magnesia sent out envoys to cities and kings requesting their recognition of the festival as crowned and *isopythian* – equal in status to the Pythian Games (*OGI* 231, 233 = Austin 184, 190). Festivals modelled upon those at Olympia and Delphi became a common feature in the Hellenistic and Roman periods, though the original festivals still remained pre-eminent in reputation. Since they belonged to the higher category of crown games it was important that other Greek cities recognised this status. While the prize at such games was a simple crown of foliage, once back home victorious athletes could expect to gain significant rewards from their cities, in the form of monetary pensions, exemption from taxes or meals at public expense (see further below, Chapter 7).

The Games at Magnesia were in honour of the city's patron deity, as was traditional in Greek culture. Yet the Hellenistic period also witnessed the arrival of a new type of festival, games held in the honour of deified kings. After the death of Alexander the Great, who had liked to view himself as the son of Zeus, and was worshipped as a god both during his lifetime and after his death, many Hellenistic kings deified their ancestors and promoted them in religious ruler cults. One such cult, that of Ptolemy I Soter ('the saviour'), the first king of Ptolemaic Egypt, was the focus for a new festival set up in Alexandria by his son and successor, Ptolemy II. Again, much of our knowledge comes from inscriptions, particularly a series of degrees in which various Greek cities or leagues formally recognise the festival, called the *Ptolemeia*, and promise to send sacred envoys to attend the sacrifices (e.g. *Syll.* 390 = Austin 218).

We also have a literary description of a lavish public procession held in Alexandria during Ptolemy II's reign. This is recorded in a work of the turn of the second to third centuries AD, the *Deipnosophistai* of Athenaios (197c-203b) – a collection of the stories supposedly told at an elite dinner party which contains many fragments from earlier writers, here the writer Kallixeinos of Rhodes. While we cannot be absolutely sure that Kallixeinos was describing the *Ptolemeia*, it seems a reasonable conclusion. The preparations made for the festival were incredibly lavish. A pavilion decorated with hanging tapestries and marble sculpture groups was set up near the palace, probably to host the delegates attending the festival, while the festival itself included several processions that threaded through the city, incorporating soldiers, priests and elaborate mythological tableaux staged on carts – in an effect perhaps not dissimilar to that of modern carnival floats. The procession of Dionysos, on which the account concentrates, even involved the distribution of free wine to those watching the procession in the stadium. All this would then have been followed on subsequent days by athletic and musical contests. Indeed, it is important to remember while we focus here on the athletic competitions, that there was much else to see at an ancient festival. As well as the contests in music, drama or chariot-racing, we sometimes hear about other performers, such as acrobats, and many orators and philosophers went to the Games to win an audience for their views. Indeed, Herodotos is said to have chosen the Olympic Games as the occasion to give a reading from his newly completed *Histories* (Lucian, *Herodotos* 1) while a Cynic philosopher of the second century AD, Peregrinos, won notoriety by publicly cremating himself at Olympia (Lucian, *The Passing of Peregrinos*).

Games in the Roman period

Festivals continued to gain in popularity during the Roman period, after a brief lapse in the first century BC when the turmoil of the civil wars in the Roman Republic led to many areas of the Greek world being used as the battlegrounds for Roman struggles for supremacy. From the first century AD onwards, rising to a peak in the second and third centuries AD, we see an explosion of festivals all around the Mediterranean world. Again the links between festivals and Greek identity seem to be an important factor here and the spread of festivals to areas such as Syria, the Lebanon and Egypt shows the keenness of cities in those areas to lay claim to Greek identity. Civic festivals were proudly proclaimed through legends on coins and public architecture (Fig. 4). They were a way to attract attention and could bring significant financial advantage in terms of the amount of trade and tourists drawn to the town.

4. A coin from Hierapolis naming the city's festival (PYTHIA) inside a wreath.

Many of these new festivals were prize games, awarding cash prizes to victors, and sometimes even offering appearance money to particular stars. This was a competitive world – with the growth of festivals across the Mediterranean smaller cities often had to use financial incentives to draw athletes to compete there. Yet a number of new crown games were also instituted in this period, either as new games, or as the upgrading of an existing festival. Now, however, the authority for granting sacred status to a festival lay in the hands of the Roman emperor. He could be petitioned by a city to award this honour and might decide to grant it as a sign of favour or gratitude for a city's loyalty. This link with the emperor explains another feature of festivals in the imperial period, the rise of those bearing the name of the imperial family. Thus we find many *Hadrianeia, Com-*

modeia and *Severeia* festivals in cities around the Greek east, showing the loyalty of individual communities to the ruling family. This does not mean that civic patron gods were downgraded. Most festivals continued to be in honour of the civic deity but also included the imperial family in their images and prayers.

A good example of the way the emperor was shown to oversee and respect a Greek civic festival can be seen in part of the relief decorating the stage wall of the theatre at Hierapolis in Asia Minor. Here the emperor Septimius Severus, seated, surrounded by all his family and crowned by the goddess of victory, Nike, presides over the city's festival in honour of its patron god Apollo. A statue of the god was originally held by the personification of the city to the left, and a large metal prize crown stands conspicuously on the table (Fig. 5).

5. This relief from the theatre at Hierapolis shows the emperor Septimius Severus presiding over the city's festival.

The Romans also adopted Greek festivals into their public spectacle culture. While we tend to hear more about the brutal gladiatorial contests of the amphitheatre or chariot-racing, Greek-style festivals with athletic and musical competitions were introduced into Rome from the middle of the first century AD. The first move had been made by the emperor Augustus, who set up the Actian Games at Nicopolis in Greece to celebrate his victory over Mark Antony and was later honoured in a festival called the *Sebasta* at Naples. Greek athletic contests were also held at Rome during his reign, in association with the 'games for the health of Caesar' voted him by the senate. But it was the emperor Nero who first introduced a full-scale Greek festival to Rome, complete with athletic, musical and equestrian competitions. This was called the *Neronia* and was held twice, in AD 60 and 65. Nero himself was a keen musician and charioteer. He participated in the *Sebasta* Games at Naples, his own *Neronia* and in the great Panhellenic games in Greece, even ordering the Olympic Games to be reorganised to fit his schedule! In general, however, elite Roman participation in the Games seems to have been frowned upon at Rome and most of those competing in the athletic contests appear to have come from the Greek world. Nero won disapproval for his exploits and the games were dropped after his death and disgrace in AD 68.

The next episode in the history of Greek festivals in Rome comes with the emperor Domitian. In AD 86 he instituted a new festival in honour of Capitoline Jupiter known as the Capitoline Games. Like the sacred games in Greece this was to be held every four years and the prize for victory was a simple wreath, apparently of oak leaves. To accommodate the contests he built an odeion (for the musical contests) and a stadium, whose traces can still be seen in Rome today in the shape of the Piazza Navona. While Domitian was also deposed and followed by a new dynasty, his festival survived to become one of the pre-eminent games of the Roman world. It is often mentioned at the top of victory lists along with the most prestigious games at Olympia, Delphi, Isthmia and Nemea. Along with the Sebasta Games at Naples, the Actian Games and the Shield Games at Argos (in honour of Hera) it also became part of a new *periodos* or circuit, complimenting the old circuit based around Olympia and Delphi. More festivals were instituted in Rome in subsequent centuries and other areas of the western empire such as Italy, Southern Gaul and North Africa followed suit.

Thus as the Greek world grew in the Hellenistic period, and then became part of the Roman Empire, its festival culture also grew. There was also a rebalancing of power. While Greek cities appealed to one another and to the various Hellenistic kings for recognition of their festivals in the Hellenistic period, later it was the Roman emperor who held the power to award the prestigious grant of sacred, crowned, status to individual festivals. In part this was because of the financial implications of having a growing number of festivals where the victors could claim exemption from public duties. Indeed, the explosion of athletic festivals meant that by the late third century AD it was necessary to limit such exemptions to those victors who had won at least three times in sacred games, including at least once in Rome or mainland Greece. However, it also served to put the emperor at the heart of a very important feature of Greek civic life, allowing him to show his concern for Greek cultural traditions while also ensuring that he was in overall control.

As this survey has shown, athletic activity certainly did not decline after the heyday of Greece in the Archaic and Classical periods. While warfare and instability affected the institution of new festivals in some periods, especially the first century BC, the revived prosperity brought by the Roman Empire encouraged individual benefactors to set up festivals for their cities around the Mediterranean. The greatest of those festivals, the Olympic Games, also continued to flourish well into the late fourth century AD. Recent excavations have yielded a bronze plaque recording the victories of two Athenian brothers in AD 381 and 385. The exact date that the Games ended is unknown. They probably ceased at the end of the fourth century, though some think they may have continued into the middle of the fifth century, when Theodosius II finally put an end to the use of pagan religious buildings in AD 435.

Chapter 6

The Setting

In order to give an idea of the setting in which the athletic competitions and festivals took place, I will here discuss just two sites; the sanctuaries at Olympia and Delphi. The appearance of these sites can be largely reconstructed through archaeological evidence, which is often clarified and brought alive by the eye-witness account of Pausanias, who records the sites as they appeared between *c.* AD 160 and 180, though he is often selective in what he chooses to record (5.10.1-6.21.3 on Olympia; 10.10.9.1-10.32.1 on Delphi). Other sites also offer interesting evidence for the history of ancient sport, in particular the well-preserved starting gates in the stadia at Isthmia and Nemea, but lack of space prevents their discussion here.

Olympia

The sanctuary at Olympia, known as the Altis, was of great antiquity, as the archaeological evidence of dedications dating back to *c.* 1000 BC has shown (see Chapter 4). While monumental adornment came later, the site had a number of natural advantages fitting it for use as a place of competition. According to a writer of the Roman imperial period, even before the Games started the river Alpheios provided water for washing and drinking, a natural plain to act as a hippodrome for horses to run in, and a valley a stade in length as a natural stadium (Philostratos, *Life of Apollonios of Tyana* 8.18). These words are heavily influenced by a desire to push the origins of the Games back into the ancient past, by presenting the site as intrinsically connected with athletic pursuits, yet they also contain a great deal of truth. The original site of the Hippodrome is lost, but was almost certainly to the south of the site in the Alpheios valley, where it was later washed away by the river in medieval times (Fig. 6). The stadium too was placed where the geography of the site provided a suitable valley. The site of the earliest stadium has been debated, but even if it did lie further to the west of its later successors, as some have claimed, its general orientation is likely to have been the same.

In the earliest days of the Games there was probably little architectural

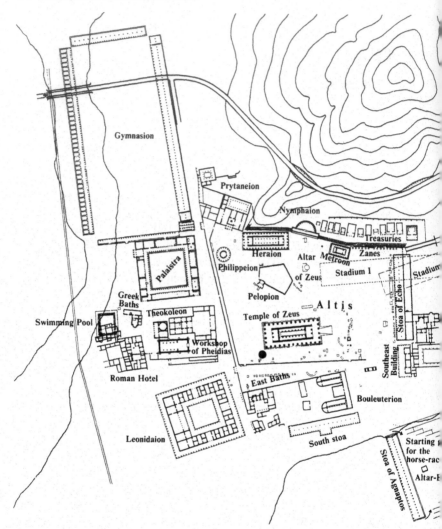

development of these spaces. Natural features were utilised instead, such as the side of the valley that provided a space for spectators in the stadium to sit. Instead, the earliest monumental buildings concentrated on the site's raison d'être – its religious role. The Temple of Hera lies to the north of the Altis and is its earliest temple. Dated to *c.* 600 BC, it originally had wooden columns, later replaced with the stone ones visible today. By Pausanias' day in the mid-second century AD the Temple was packed with dedications from various individuals and states (5.17.1-5.20.3). As well as setting up dedications in the Temples of Hera or Zeus, some cities built

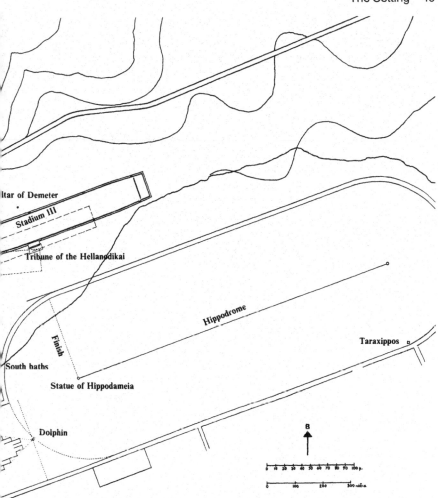

6. Plan of the Sanctuary at Olympia.

miniature structures to house their dedications, now usually called Treasuries, in a line on the terrace to the north of the Altis.

Just to the south of the Temple of Hera lay the Pelopion, a shrine to the hero Pelops, which in the early fourth century BC seems to have consisted of a mound surrounded by an enclosure wall. To the east of the Pelopion lay the Altar of Zeus, a massive construction formed from the ashes of previous sacrifices of which nothing survives today (it is described by Pausanias, 5.13.8). The Temple of Zeus lay further to the south and was completed in 456 BC.

Interpretation of the archaeological findings is helped by the clear description given by Pausanias (5.10.1-10). He describes the subjects of the pediments – the chariot race between Pelops and Oinomaos on the eastern pediment, facing towards the stadium, and the battle between the Centaurs and Lapiths on the west side. The metopes were decorated with scenes of the labours of Herakles. The cult statue was added around 430 BC. It was the work of the Athenian Pheidias, who also completed the statue of Athena in the Parthenon at Athens, and was chryselephantine – in ivory and gold. It showed Zeus seated on a throne and holding the figure of Nike (Victory) in his right hand. The size and magnificence of the statue became legendary, and in the Hellenistic period it was counted as one of the Seven Wonders of the Ancient World. Pheidias' workshop has been found in the excavations, in a building later converted into a Christian church.

According to Pausanias, the Temple of Zeus was dedicated by the Eleans from the spoils they had won in a battle over their rival Pisa (Pausanias 5.10.2). Indeed, the whole sanctuary was filled with dedications attesting to military victories. Dedications of helmets have been found at the site, while excavations in the stadium show that trophies of captured armour were set up in the seating area. Olympia was a key Panhellenic gathering place, yet as well as bringing the Greeks together it also provided them with a showplace to advertise their victories over one another. Boasts of military superiority were also echoed in the many statues set up by cities to their successful athletes that thronged the spaces between buildings in the Altis (see Chapter 7).

As the site of a famous festival, which attracted competitors and spectators from across the Greek world, we might expect to find facilities for accommodation, bathing and training. In fact such amenities were added only rather late to the site. Literary accounts record complaints about the discomfort involved in a trip to Olympia such as the heat, cramped conditions and lack of adequate bathing facilities (Epictetus, *Discourse* 1.6.23-8 = *Arete* 146). Over time, however, some amenities were added. The fourth-century BC Leonidaion to the south-west of the site was probably a guest house for elite visitors and a gymnasium for the athletes was added in the third century BC. Building also continued throughout the Roman period, such as the clubhouse to the south of the Altis which was begun by Nero and finished under Domitian. Many visitors, however, must have simply camped in the surrounding area and made do as best they could. Indeed, it was not until the second century AD that Olympia received a permanent water supply in the form of an elaborate nymphaeum (fountain) funded by the Athenian notable Herodes

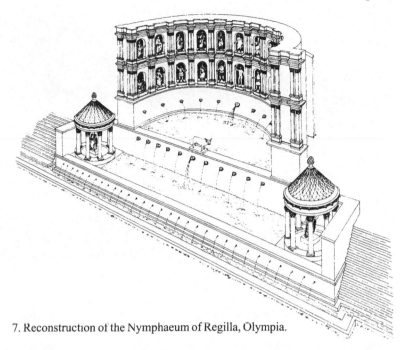

7. Reconstruction of the Nymphaeum of Regilla, Olympia.

Attikos and dedicated by his wife Regilla, the priestess of Demeter at Olympia (Fig. 7). In earlier times temporary wells had been dug to provide for the festival.

Delphi

A similar mixture of religious structures, dedications and buildings to accommodate the contests can be seen at Delphi, though their topography makes the two sites appear very different. Here the sanctuary is built on a hillside, with the Temple of Apollo at its heart. Along the road leading up to the Temple are a number of treasuries. As at Olympia, dedications were often used to celebrate victories in battle as in the Stoa of the Athenians which bears an inscription identifying the ships' prows displayed there as enemy trophies from their victory over the Persians at Salamis in 480 BC.

The areas for competition lie above and below the main area of the sanctuary. Since the Pythian Games included musical contests as well as athletics, a theatre was built just to the north-west of the temple. A stadium was also constructed at the top of the sanctuary in the third century BC though the athletic contests may have taken place in the valley below in

8. View of the stadium at Delphi, as reconstructed in the second century AD by Herodes Attikos.

earlier periods. The valley was also the location for the hippodrome as well as a gymnasium complex. The stadium was rebuilt in the second century AD by Herodes Attikos (Fig. 8). This was one of his many acts of generosity to Panhellenic centres. In addition to the nymphaeum at Olympia, mentioned above, he also built an odeion at Corinth and dedicated new cult statues at Isthmia, in addition to building a stadium and odeion at Athens, his home city, for the celebration of the Panathenaia. The fact that wealthy benefactors like Herodes often chose either to found new festivals or fund the buildings associated with them shows the enduring importance of festival and athletic culture within Greek civic life throughout history, even during the period of the Roman Empire.

Chapter 7

The Rewards for Victory

The prizes for victory in the various contests have already been outlined above (Chapter 5). While prizes of money or valuable objects could be given in some games, the most prestigious awarded a simple wreath. However, this wreath could bring with it a whole host of other benefits that the athlete would gain on his return home. In Archaic Athens Solon is said to have set down the amount of money payable to Panhellenic victors at 500 drachmae for Olympic victors and 100 for Isthmian victors (Plutarch, *Solon*, 23.2 = *Arete* 223) while by the fifth century BC these victors could claim free meals for the rest of their lives at public expense (*IG* 1 131 = *Arete* 221). Other honours could include a triumphal entrance into the city as well as immunity from public duties – many of which bore a financial cost.

Yet in addition to the financial rewards of victory, athletes also won something much more pervasive – everlasting glory. Through statues and victory odes their achievements could be recorded for posterity to leave a tangible record that still survives today. Sometimes these records were commissioned and paid for by the athlete himself or his family or trainer. Often, however, they were funded by his city, as a proud record of its ability to produce a Panhellenic champion.

Pindar and the athletic victory ode

One of the most prestigious and enduring forms of commemoration of a victory was an ode, commissioned by the athlete or his family or city, and performed either at the site of his victory or on his return home. The poet best known for this form of commemoration is Pindar, whose odes in honour of victors at Olympia, Delphi, Isthmia and Nemea have survived to this day, proving his claims that a victory ode can span space and time to give everlasting glory to its honorand (*Nemean* 5.1-4; *Isthmian* 4.57-8).

Pindar was not the only poet to compose such hymns of praise. Recent papyrus finds have shown that the poet Ibykos of Rhegium was composing victory odes by the middle of the sixth century BC, and he was followed by the poets Simonides and later Bacchylides, a contemporary of Pindar.

Like these poets, Pindar also composed other sorts of works too, such as hymns in honour of the gods or poems sung at aristocratic symposia, but it is his victory, or 'epinician' odes (from the Greek word for Victory, *nike*) that have survived and for which he is most famous. Pindar was born towards the end of the sixth century BC and his odes span the whole of the first half of the fifth century. Most of them seem to have been performed in a victor's hometown, perhaps on his triumphant return from the Games or during a symposium in his honour (as is suggested by the opening of *Olympian* 7, in honour of Diagoras of Rhodes). The recipients of the odes include members of the aristocracy of various Greek cities and islands as well as tyrants and autocrats, in particular the rulers of Sicily such as Hieron of Syracuse (*Olympian* 1, *Pythian* 1, 2, 3) and Theron of Akragas (*Olympian* 2, 3). Other poets were also active at the courts of these men, including Simonides and his nephew Bacchylides, and indeed when Hieron won the chariot race at Olympia in 468 BC it was Bacchylides rather than Pindar whom he chose to compose his victory ode (Bacchylides, *Ode* 3).

The victories won by these rulers were primarily in equestrian contests such as the horse and mule chariot races. To be able to raise and train a stable of successful horses was a mark of great wealth and power and these victories could be recorded both in epinician odes and in sculptural groups set up at Olympia or the other Panhellenic sanctuaries (see below). Some of the odes honouring members of the aristocracy also celebrate equestrian victories but many record athletic victories in the wrestling, boxing or foot races. Sometimes, especially for young athletes, the victories of other members of his family or even his trainer might be alluded to.

Olympian 8 celebrates the victory of Alkimedon of Aegina in the boys' wrestling at Olympia in 460 BC and includes praise of the athlete's trainer, Melesias, as well as the athlete himself and his family. Melesias too had won victories in his youth, including the pancration at Nemea, and Alkimedon's victory over four rivals is said to have brought him his thirtieth victory. In general, however, Pindar avoids describing the victories at any length, simply working in a reference to the contest at some point in the poem. Occasionally this can come at the start of the ode, as in *Olympian* 5 which begins by asking the athlete's home city of Kamarina in Sicily to accept the ode as the reward for 'the crowns won at Olympia, the gifts of Psaumis and his chariot team on their untiring course'. Within the first four lines of the poem Pindar identifies the name and city of the victor, the contest and the place where it has been won. Often, however, this information is instead revealed piecemeal in the main body of the poem after an opening asking for attention or praising the place where the victory was achieved.

One characteristic of Pindar's odes which has attracted much scholarly attention is his extensive use of myth. Indeed, while he skates over the details of the victories actually achieved, Pindar describes various mythical episodes in great detail. These mythical allusions often contribute to the honour of the victor by providing a mythical analogy to the victory or lauding his family's ancestry. Thus the description of the myth of Pelops in *Olympian* 1 exalts Hieron by providing a mythical example of equestrian prowess, and tactfully ignores the version of the myth in which Pelops' chariot victory was achieved by bribing Myrtilos to sabotage Oinomaos' chariot (although if this version originates with Sophokles' *Oinomaos*, as some suspect, it would not yet have been current). In *Olympian* 7 the mythical interlude serves instead to praise the ancestry of the victor, Diagoras of Rhodes, by tracing this back via Tlepolemos to Herakles himself, as well as praising his home island of Rhodes.

Praise of the victor's city as well as his own achievements was an important feature to include. The athletic achievements of the aristocracy could be seen as a potential threat, leading to over-confidence and threatening upheaval of the political system. By setting the victor's achievement in the wider context of his city's own prestigious past Pindar could help to neutralise this risk, using the victor's success as a way of praising his city, rather than as a threat to it. This could not always be achieved. *Pythian* 7 begins with praise of the victor's home city of Athens as the most glorious in Greece, but laments the fact that the rewards for Megakles' success (in chariot-racing) are the 'wounds of envy' (*Pythian* 7.18). Megakles came from the aristocratic Alkmaionid family and Pindar here seems to be referring to his ostracism from the city. His wealth and prestige were perhaps seen as a threat to the fledging democracy of Athens.

In other poems Pindar uses myths differently, perhaps to illustrate the origins of the festival where the victory had been won (e.g. *Olympian* 10). In all these cases, however, we can see the mythical element not simply as a digression or decoration, but as an essential means of achieving the poem's aim – to commemorate the victor's achievement by comparing it with the greatest deeds of the mythical past. Yet while the victor is thus implicitly compared to heroes and gods, it was also important to remember that he was only mortal, even if his victory and its commemoration in song or marble could bring a sort of immortality. As balance to the aggrandisement suggested by the mythical elements of the odes, we also find warnings about knowing one's own limits and avoiding the envy incurred by excessive pride. So *Olympian* 5 ends with the warning to Psaumis to use his wealth wisely and 'not seek to become a god' (*Olympian* 5.24) while other odes warn of the changeability of fortune or the necessity of combining success with honourable behaviour.

Athletic victory statues

Another way in which an athlete might be commemorated was through art, in statues set up either at the place of victory or in the athlete's home town. The overcrowded Altis at Olympia in second century AD, crammed with victory monuments dating back into the Archaic past, is vividly shown through Pausanias' lengthy description of the statues he saw here (6.1.1-6.18.7). Many of these can be identified in the archaeological record from their inscribed bases. Victors in the chariot race often chose to set up a record of their achievement in the form of a chariot group, such as that set up by the Spartan princess Kyniska at Olympia (above, Chapter 2). One famous example of such a dedication is the Delphic charioteer (Fig. 9), part of a chariot group set up by Polyzalos of Gela in 478 or 474 BC. Polyzalos himself was perhaps represented elsewhere in the monument, but the only part that survives is the figure of the hired charioteer, dressed in the characteristic long gown. Another statue that may have originally formed part of a memorial to a chariot victory was found in Sicily and is known as the Motya youth (Fig. 10). Like the Delphic figure he too wears a long robe, but the diaphanous drapery here clings to the youth's body, outlining the athletic physique below, possibly a sign that this represents the owner himself, who had personally acted as charioteer.

Victories in the athletic contests could be recorded either in action poses, or in statues showing the athlete after his victory, for example, while he was being crowned. Most of the victory statues created in the Classical period have been lost, melted down for the value of their bronze or otherwise destroyed over the passage of time. However, glimpses of them can be seen in the idealising sculpture produced during the Roman period, some of which directly copied Classical masterpieces. Past scholars have often been overzealous in identifying a statue that was popular in the Roman period as a Classical statue mentioned in the literary record. However, in some cases we can be certain that these statues were copying Greek predecessors. One famous example is Myron's Diskobolos, a statue that was a popular choice in the Roman period for the decoration of villas, baths and gymnasia (Fig. 11). It is clearly described in a passage by Lucian, writing in the second century AD, as follows:

'You don't mean the discus-thrower', I said, 'the one bent over in

9. The Delphic charioteer, part of a victory monument set up at Delphi.

10. The 'Motya youth', a marble statue of a charioteer.

the position of the throw, turned back towards the hand that holds the discus, with one leg slightly bent, as if he would spring up at once with the cast?' 'Not that one', said he, 'for you are talking about one of Myron's works, the discus-thrower (*diskobolos*). Nor do I mean the one beside it, the one binding his head with a fillet

(*ton diadoumenon*), the beautiful lad, for that is Polykleitos' work.'
(Lucian, *Lover of Lies* 18)

Both the statues mentioned here can be identified in Roman copies, and they illustrate the two different types of statue outlined above. The Diskobolos shows the athlete just as he is about to cast the discus from him, whereas the Diadoumenos shows the victorious athlete after his contest, as he ties a ribbon of victory around his head. The original statues probably commemorated victories won at a Panhellenic festival; from

11. Roman copy of Myron's Diskobolos statue, found at Hadrian's Villa at Tivoli, Italy. The head is restored incorrectly, and would originally have been turned back to look at the hand with the discus.

12. Roman copy of Polykleitos' Doryphoros statue.

literary and epigraphical evidence we know that both artists undertook commissions at sites such as Olympia and Delphi. The Diskobolos statue ought to commemorate a pentathlete. By showing the discus throw, a competition that did not take place as a contest in its own right at Olympia, the artist is able to indicate the victor's field. Yet the names of these victors, inscribed on the bases of the original statues, are now lost to us. By the Roman period they had become valued instead for their generic qualities, as examples of a 'discus-thrower' and 'man binding his head' rather than 'X, son of Y, from Z who won the pentathlon in the nth Olympiad'. The anonymity of these statues means that we cannot be absolutely sure that they were originally set up as victory monuments.

Some have seen them instead as genre pieces, or as mythological scenes – Apollo about to cast the fatal throw of the discus that will kill his beloved Hyacinth, for example.

A similar ambiguity haunts one of the most famous works of Classical sculpture, Polykleitos' Doryphoros, also known only through later copies (Fig. 12). Again scholars are uncertain – did Polykleitos create the piece as a purely artistic enterprise, to represent his *kanon* – the ideal proportions of the naked male body? Or does the statue commemorate a victorious pentathlete, with the javelin he held acting as a sign of that contest, just as the discus does in Myron's statue? Or, in fact, should we identify this not as a javelin but as a spear, indicating that the figure is a warrior? If so, he might be a mythological warrior, the famous Achilles. Much of our uncertainty is down to the Roman writers who were similarly vague, seeing the statue as, in Quintilian's words 'equally suited for warfare or the palaestra' (*Institutio Oratoria* 5.12.21).

While on the subject of uncertainty, it might be time to mention the hoary chestnut of 'iconic statues'. Pliny the Elder tells us in his *Natural History*, written in the mid-first century AD, that only those who had been victorious three times at Olympia were awarded the status of statues 'forged in the image of their own limbs, which they call iconic' (*Natural History* 34.16). This seems to suggest that the statues were portraits of their victors, but many of the copies seem to have idealised features rather than portrait faces. Some suggest that *iconicas* may instead have meant showing the athletics with attributes of the contest in which they had won their victory, rather than with portrait features.

Despite the gaps in our knowledge, we can piece together much of the character of this commemorative statuary. In style and tone it seems to have followed the artistic trends of the time. Archaic victories were celebrated by the erection of *kouroi*, like those set up at other sanctuaries or as tomb markers. Classical statues seem to have been marked by a calmness and modesty, especially in the faces of youthful victors, though the surviving evidence from Roman copies might also be influenced by the Roman liking for images of modest boys. In contrast, the Hellenistic period seems to have introduced more realistic figures that show the damage the violent contests of boxing and the pancration could wreak on the bodies of contestants. A wonderful head which survives from Olympia shows the cauliflower ears and scars of a boxer, while the seated boxer in Rome also stresses the exhaustion of the athlete once his fight is won (Fig. 13).

13. Hellenistic bronze statue of a boxer.

Chapter 8

The Athlete and his City

As mentioned above, victorious athletes could expect to receive financial rewards from their cities for victories gained at the most prestigious festivals, and often had their victory statues funded by the state. The close link between Panhellenic success and civic prestige can be seen in a speech written by Isokrates for the son of the famous Athenian politician, Alkibiades. Here the son draws attention to the victories his father had won in the chariot race at Olympia, and declares them to be a form of public benefaction:

> He believed that public services here were to the credit of the individual in the eyes of the citizens, but that services at that festival [Olympia] were to the credit of the city in the eyes of the whole of Greece ... Therefore he tried his hand at horse breeding ... and beat not only his competitors but all those who had ever been victors previously. (Isokrates, *Team of Horses* 32-3 = *Arete* 67)

Alkibiades' decision to compete at the Olympic Games is shown to be a patriotic act.

Of course, the arguments presented here are cut to fit the defence of the elder Alkibiades, but plentiful other evidence survives to show the honour in which successful athletes were held by their cities. In addition to having statues set up at sanctuaries such as Olympia or Delphi, athletes were also represented by statues within their own cities. These could be displayed in religious sanctuaries or other public spaces. Thus the athletes Epicharinos and Hermolykos had statues on the Athenian acropolis (Pausanias 1.23.9-10) while a statue of the famous fifth-century athlete Promachos still stood as an example to the young in the gymnasium at Pellene in the imperial period (Pausanias 7.27.5). The city of Megara preserved the tomb of one famous athlete in their agora. This was the eighth-century runner Orsippos (or Orrhippos) who was commemorated on his tomb as being the first athlete to run naked at Olympia (Pausanias 1.44.1; *IG* VII, 52).

The inscription on Orsippos' tomb was carefully preserved, and had probably been re-inscribed around the time that Pausanias viewed it. Preserving the memory of past Olympic victors seems to have been of great importance to the cities of the Greek east in the Roman Empire, a period when these cities often relied on their prestigious pasts to gain status in the contemporary world. The fact that Pausanias draws attention to the statues of Panhellenic victors which continue to adorn Greek cities shows the continuing importance of this link between cities and their victors.

One of the ways this link was expressed was through the heroisation of athletic victors. A number of victorious athletes are known to have received heroic honours. One famous example is the fifth-century BC athlete Theagenes of Thasos who won fame for his phenomenal strength and his huge number of athletic victories, which is given as 1,400. His story is told by Pausanias (6.11.2-9). After Theagenes' death an enemy of his is said to have wreaked his revenge by flogging the athlete's statue as if it were Theagenes himself. The statue retaliated by falling on the man and killing him, with the result that it was accused of murder by the Thasians and dropped into the sea. When famine fell upon the city and envoys were sent to Delphi, the oracle urged the Thasians to recall their exiles, a command which was finally understood to mean retrieving Theagenes' statue. Once this was recovered and honoured with sacrifices by the Thasians, Theagenes finally received his due recognition.

A number of the stories of the heroisation of athletes cluster around the late sixth and early fifth centuries BC, and it has been suggested that the practice developed in times of civic unrest, perhaps as a means of balancing the fame and prestige of these elite athletes with the needs of the *polis*. Once instituted these heroic honours continued well into the Roman period, and indeed much of our evidence comes precisely from this period. Theagenes is mentioned by Lucian (*Parliament of the Gods* 12) and Dio Chrysostom (*Oration* 31.95-9) as well as Pausanias, and an offering box found at Thasos and dated to around 100 AD also provides archaeological evidence for the continuity of his worship into imperial times (*Arete* 167b).

Another story about the importance of cities honouring their athletes appropriately is again recorded by Pausanias. This time the athlete is called Oibotas, and comes from the small town of Dyme in the Peloponnese. Oibotas was a victor in the sixth Olympic games of 756 BC, but his statue at Olympia was not erected until 460 BC (Pausanias 6.3.8). Pausanias tells us that although Oibotas was the first Achaian to win a victory at Olympia, he had not received proper recognition for this victory. He promptly made a curse that no other Achaian in future should win an

Olympic victory. Finally the Achaians asked the god at Delphi why they had been so unsuccessful. Once they learnt the reason they started to honour Oibotas and set up a statue to him at Olympia. An Achaian athlete, Sostratos of Pellene, then promptly won the *stadion* race for boys. Even in his own time, Pausanias says, it was the custom for Achaian athletes going to compete at Olympia first to sacrifice to Oibotas as a hero and, if they won, to crown his statue at Olympia (7.17.13-14).

These stories show the importance attached to a city properly honouring her victorious athletes, and to the prestigious position some athletes could win. As well as receiving offerings, heroised athletes were also credited with having the power to heal others and to help them onto victory. Yet the honour which a city granted its athletes also involved obligations. When the athlete Astylos of Kroton decided on his second and third Olympic appearances to renounce his city and declare himself a citizen of Syracuse (probably at the behest of the tyrant of Syracuse, Hieron), his home city took revenge. They turned his house into a prison and took down the statue of him in the sanctuary of Hera Lakinia (Pausanias 6.13.1). Astylus' obliteration of Kroton through choosing to be heralded as a citizen of a different city was punished by the obliteration of his images back at home.

Stories such as these suggest that athletes could be a useful tool in struggles for status and supremacy between rival cities. Even in the placement of the statues at Olympia we get a sense of these rivalries being played out. When the Spartans in the fifth century BC commissioned the sculptor Myron to construct a statue of their famous runner Chionis, whose victories had taken place in the seventh century BC, they also erected a stele pointing out that at the period he was victorious the race in armour had not yet been introduced to the Olympic programme (Pausanias 6.13.2). This seems to be a deliberate response to the nearby statue of Astylos of Kroton, who had won in this contest as well, as a pre-emptive strike against anyone who might dare to say that Sparta's athlete was inferior. Just as other monuments set up in the Altis at Olympia proclaimed military victories over rival cities, so too athletic victories could be used by cities as a key weapon in their struggles for supremacy.

Not everyone approved of the honours that were granted to these victorious athletes. A fragment of the writings of the philosopher Xenophanes, from around 525 BC, criticises the current custom of praising athletic strength: such victories do not help to ensure justice in a city, nor to improve her financial position. Instead, he states, wisdom ought to be valued more than the physical strength of men or horses (Xenophanes, fragment 2 = *Arete* 229). Similar sentiments are expressed about a century later in a play by Euripides, though the fragmentary nature of the text means that we should be careful before ascribing the views to Euripides himself – they might, instead, have been part of his characterisation of a particular figure. Here the anonymous speaker first curses the race of athletes as being the greatest evil in Greece, and scornfully rejects any notion that they can help to defend the city during warfare. Instead, he argues 'we ought to crown the wise man, the just, whoever best leads the city, being moderate and just' (Euripides, *Autolykos*, fragment 282.23-5 = *Arete* 230).

This strand of criticism, with its argument that rather than praising physical prowess the city would be better advised to reward intellectual and philosophical qualities, survived well into the Roman period. The medical writer Galen expresses concern lest the youth of his day be beguiled by the praises heaped upon athletes into thinking that this is a worthy art to study – instead he urges them towards more intellectual pursuits, including the study of medicine (Galen, *Exhortation to Study the Arts* 9 = *Arete* 215). Of course, Xenophanes and Galen have their own self-interest at heart – the desire to promote their own area of study and to praise intellectual pursuits over physical ones.

Chapter 9

The Rise of Professionalism?

In the speech by Isokrates mentioned above, the younger Alkibiades explains why his father chose to compete in the chariot-racing rather than in one of the athletic competitions:

> Though in no ways untalented nor weak of body, he scorned gymnastic games since he knew that some of the athletes were low-born and from small city states and badly educated. (Isokrates, *Team of Horses* 33)

This comment brings us to one of the key areas of debate in the study of Greek athletics – the social status of the participants. The traditional picture has long suggested that in the earliest days of the Games athletics was a pursuit of the aristocracy, who alone had the time and wealth to devote themselves to training. Over time, however, figures from a wider social spectrum began to take part in the Games, with the result that by the late fifth century BC Alkibiades could scorn those taking part in the Olympic Games as being of low birth. This picture of Greek athletics has been closely intertwined with the Victorian notion of a distinction be-tween 'professional' and 'amateur' athletes (see Chapter 1 above). Whereas the aristocracy of Archaic Greece had no need for valuable prizes and competed simply for the glory of victory, the argument goes, as time went on a class of 'professional' athletes emerged, who toured the athletic circuit and made themselves rich on their winnings at prize games. According to this view, by the Roman period athletics had been thor-oughly professionalised, occupied solely by these career athletes and no longer being the pursuit of elite gentlemen.

Recent research had challenged this picture, but it is useful to draw out the two strands that tend to become intertwined here. On the one hand is the social status and wealth of the athletes – whether or not athletics changed from being an upper-class to a lower-class activity over time. One the other lie the rewards for victory – the ideal of amateurism where competitors compete for glory rather than money, versus that of the professional career athlete who tours the festivals of Greece making his fortune along the way. These tend to become linked, with the result that the wealthy aristocrat is seen as an amateur while the professional career athlete must have been lower class. Yet there is no reason why these associations must be true and it is better to look at these two aspects – class and professionalism – separately.

Thus, as recent research has shown, even the earliest athletes can be seen as professionals, if that means the amount of time they devoted to their athletic careers. Theagenes of Thasos is credited with having won 1,400 victories. Even if this figure is exaggerated it is surely a sign that he must have dedicated a substantial part of his youth to training and competition. Theagenes seems to have belonged to an important family and his father acted as priest of Herakles in his home city. Another famous athlete who made a career out of athletics is the wrestler Milon of Kroton, said to have competed seven times at Olympia, that is over a period of 28 years! He too probably came from an elite family and played an important role in his city's military campaign against Sybaris. A recent attempt to challenge the traditional picture of early athletes as elite amateurs has sought to show that low-class athletes were victorious at Olympia even from the beginning, such as the 'cook' Koroibos, victor in the very first games, or the boxer Glaukos who won his victory after recalling a time in his youth when he beat a ploughshare into shape with his bare hands. Yet the word for cook (*mageiros*) might also mean someone who presides at a sacrifice, a relatively high-ranking position, and Glaukos' experience of farming may actually imply his membership of a wealthy, land-owning family. The picture of elite athletes competing in the earliest games still seems to hold weight, though the idea that they were occasional amateurs rather than fully dedicated to spending a significant proportion of their youth pursuing athletic success can probably now be discounted.

What about the idea that athletics became more professional in later centuries and also admitted competitors from a lower social background? Again the two things need to be distinguished. There is certainly evidence of an increasingly organised approach to festival culture in the Hellenistic and Roman periods. Thus as the number of festivals increased we also see the rise of professional guilds supporting the interests of performers. From the third century BC a guild of actors called the Artists of Dionysos is known to have sought protection and privileges for its members first from the Hellenistic kings and then later from the Roman emperors. An athletic guild, the 'synod of international sacred victors' is also known from the first century BC, when it secured for its members the right to exemption from military services and public liturgies (public services with a financial obligation). This guild later seems to have been associated particularly with the athletic hero Herakles, and in the second century AD set up its headquarters at Rome.

Yet the appearance of guilds need not imply that all athletes were of low-class origin. Indeed, when one looks at the officials who ran the guild we find that as well as being victorious athletes in their youth they often seem to have held important positions in numerous cities. Thus an inscription honouring the Alexandrian athlete Marcus Aurelius Asklepiades, also known as Hermodoros, tells us that he was a citizen of Alexandria, Hermopolis and Puteoli and acted as a member of the council (*boule*) in Naples, Elis and Athens among other cities, before going on to list his numerous victories in the pancration (*IG* XIV 1102, from Rome = *Arete* 213). While it is certainly possible that some lower-class athletes worked their way up the social ladder through their athletic victories, there is plentiful evidence to suggest that the elites of cities in the eastern part of the Roman Empire were keen to advertise any athletic victories that their relatives had won. An inscription in the stadium at Aizanoi in Asia Minor celebrates the achievements of various members of the family of one M. Ulpius Appuleius Eurykles, including the Olympic victory won by his wife's grandfather in AD 93. Another elite athlete, Lucius Septimius Flavianus Flavillianus of Oinoanda in Lykia, won numerous victories in wrestling and the pancration and was also mentioned on a genealogical inscription carved onto his aunt's tomb. These two examples show that the elites of the cities of Asia Minor were proud to be related to athletic victors, and that elite athletes continued to compete at festivals from Archaic to Roman times. While some middle or lower-class athletes could have gained prestige and wealth through their victories, they would have needed financial support to be able to invest in the time and training necessary for this success. We do have some evidence of wealthy citizens supporting promising athletes from the Hellenistic period (*PZenon* 59060 = *Arete* 207), but the traditional picture of the aristocracy gradually abandoning athletics to the lower classes can be categorically rejected.

The modern terms of amateurism and professionalism simply do not make sense when applied to the ancient world. To compete successfully at any period required a substantial investment of time and the wealth necessary initially to afford this leisure and to pay for travel and training. We have also seen that athletes at all periods could make substantial amounts of money from their victories, whether in the form of valuable cash prizes, or from the benefits offered by their home cities as a reward for victories at the prestigious sacred games. Over time there does seem to have been the development of an athletic industry, with the institution of guilds to protect athletes' rights and rewards and with the introduction of increasingly specialised training regimes. For the Roman period we hear from Philostratos of the controversial *tetrada*, a four-day training schedule that he criticises as harmful (*Gymnastikos* 54), though Philostratos has his own advice on how athletes should be trained. The medical writer Galen was more sceptical, criticising the diet and lifestyle of athletes and warning of the dangers they expose themselves to (Galen, *Exhortation to Study the Arts* 9-14 = *Arete* 215). Strict diets and regimes were also thought to be a feature of athletics in earlier periods too. Pausanias credits the athlete Dromeus with having transformed the athletic diet from one of cheese to meat (Pausanias 6.7.10) and Athenaios records the excessive appetite of the earlier athlete, Milon of Kroton (*Deipnosophistai* 10.412f).

Part II

The World of the Gymnasium

Chapter 10

The Origins and Development of the Gymnasium

By the Hellenistic and Roman periods the gymnasium had become a defining characteristic of a Greek city. Indeed Pausanias mocks the obscure city of Panopeus in Phokis, saying that it was hardly worthy of the name of city when it did not possess any of the requisite structures – government buildings, gymnasium, theatre or agora (Pausanias 10.4.1). However, the origins of this key institution are rather more obscure and our earliest surviving archaeological examples go back only as far as the fourth century BC. It seems clear, however, that the gymnasium as a place where men went to exercise naked (it takes its name from the Greek for naked, *gymnos*) developed in the sixth century BC. The archaic poet Theognis declared 'happy the lover who spends time in the gymnasium/athletic pursuits (*gymnazetai*) and, returning home, enjoys the whole day with a handsome youth' (*Elegy* B, 11.1335-6). The sixth-century tyrant of Samos, Polykrates, was later said to have burnt down the gymnasium at Samos because it encouraged relationships that undermined his tyranny (Athenaios, *Deipnosophistai* 13.602d). We will look more closely at this linking of the gymnasium with homosexual courtship in Chapter 12, but what both these sources suggest is that the gymnasium as a place for men to spend their leisure time was in existence by the middle of the sixth century BC.

The earlier sixth century was precisely the time that the Panhellenic festivals at Delphi, Isthmia and Nemea were instituted, as well as the Panathenaic games at Athens, and it seems reasonable to link the development of a place known as the gymnasium with the rise in athletic training and competition necessitated by these festivals. An alternative view would suggest that the development of the gymnasium should be associated with the rise of hoplite warfare, based around the use of heavily-armed infantry, hoplites, marching in close formation. However, rather than being devised as a place for training in this new form of warfare, it is possible that the gymnasium (and the newly founded festivals) provided the elite with a space in which to express their physical prowess and superiority, when the changes in warfare away from single combat had deprived them of that particular stage for their ambitions. The links between the gymnasium and elite culture are also suggested by the appearance of scenes from the gymnasium on Athenian pottery, particularly on vessels which were used in the symposium. Exercise in the gymnasium and involvement in elite drinking parties seem to have been pursuits shared by the same aristocratic members of society.

The form that these early gymnasia took can only be reconstructed from literary evidence, but for Athens we have records of at least three archaic gymnasia, the Akademia (Academy), Lykeion (Lyceum) and Kynosarges. A link with the development of festivals is suggested by the fact that the Peisistratids (tyrants of Athens in the later sixth century BC) are credited with involvement both in the reorganisation of the Panathenaia and in the construction or embellishment of gymnasia. Hipparchos is said to have built a wall around the Academy while Peisistratos may have founded the Lyceum, though other sources attribute this to Perikles or Lykourgos. From descriptions of these complexes in later sources they seem to have included large areas of open space for walking and running. References to Solon prescribing penalties for theft from these gymnasia and to regulations concerning their opening times suggest that they were enclosed by walls rather than simply consisting of open park land (Demosthenes, *Against Timocrates* 114; Aeschines, *Against Timarchos* 10). They were also associated with shrines to particular heroes. Indeed the Academy took its name from the hero Akademos while the Lyceum was sacred to Apollo Lykeios.

Literary sources mention the existence of palaestrai as well as gymnasia, and the differences between the two have exercised scholars over the years. At times it seems as if the two terms can be used interchangeably as places where men go to exercise. The names of the two complexes certainly imply a link with athletic activity – the gymnasium as a place for naked athletic activity and the palaestra as a place for wrestling (from *pale*, the Greek for wrestling). However, there are also some cases in which a distinction does seem to be drawn between the two. In general it seems that gymnasia were usually publicly-funded institutions, open to all citizens, whereas palaestrai are often presented as private enterprises which may also have had a more limited clientele. Gymnasia often seem to be bigger too, including areas for walking and running as well as structures for wrestling or boxing. Indeed, sometimes we hear of a gymnasium that includes a palaestra, in which case the gymnasium refers to the complex as a whole whereas the palaestra part is made up of a portico surrounding an open court with its associated rooms for dressing, chatting and washing. Some establishments seem to have been limited to specific groups, such as boys, youths or adult men, and indeed the gymnasium was an important site for the education of citizen youths, as we will see below. In general, then, it is often impossible to be precisely sure what an author means by gymnasium or palaestra, but in all cases these complexes seem to have combined rooms for conversation and discussion with areas for washing, dressing and massage as well as areas to practice the various different athletic activities.

From the later fifth century BC, in Athens at least, the gymnasium also became closely associated with other forms of education such as philosophical discussions. Indeed, in Plato's dialogues it is often to the gymnasium that Sokrates goes when seeking people to engage in debate. The *Euthydemos* is set in the dressing room of the Lyceum, while the *Lysis* is set in a private newly-opened palaestra. Later philosophers also chose to base themselves in particular gymnasia. Plato was associated with the Academy and Aristotle with the Lyceum – with the result that those names, which initially referred to the heroes or gods associated with the areas, have now become used instead as terms for places of education.

The place for nakedness

As we have seen, the name of the gymnasium comes from the Greek word *gymnos*, naked. As is well known, the Greeks were accustomed to exercise naked, a custom that differentiated them from other groups such as the Etruscans or Romans who customarily wore loincloths. Even for the Greeks themselves the origins of this custom were unclear, though they believed that they had not always exercised naked and that earlier athletes, like those in Homer, wore a loincloth. For Thucydides (1.6.5), writing around 420 BC, it was 'not many years ago' that the practice of exercising naked had arisen. He attributes it to the Spartans and says that in the earliest Olympic Games athletes used to wear a loincloth, as indeed non-Greeks in Asia still did in his day. An alternative view, however, attributed the origins of the custom not to the Spartans but to Orsippos of Megara, and indeed his tombstone proudly proclaimed the fact that he was the first Greek to be crowned at Olympia naked, when all previous stade runners had worn loincloths (*IG* VII, 52). Pausanias (1.44.1) suggests that the loss of his loincloth was deliberate, and that Orsippos realised that he could run more easily unencumbered by clothing. According to this tradition, the origins of athletic nudity would belong in 720 BC, the year in which Orsippos won at Olympia. Dionysios of Halikarnassos also gave this as the date for the origins of athletic nudity, though he, like Thucydides, attributed it to a Spartan, the runner Akanthos (7.72.2-3). While Thucydides' 'not long since' might suggest that the custom originated in

14. Vase painting showing athletes engaged in boxing and the pancration, and a clothed trainer carrying a whip.

the late sixth or early fifth century BC, naked athletes appear on vases and in *kouroi* statues long before then and it seems likely that an earlier date should be preferred.

In the images of the gymnasium that appear on vases, trainers in the gymnasium are usually shown clothed, and often carry a whip to punish transgressions of the rules (Fig. 14). At Olympia, however, we hear that they were also required to appear naked. According to Pausanias, one year the mother of an athlete disguised herself as a trainer in order to watch her son perform (married women, with the exception of the priestess of Demeter, were excluded from the games). When her son won his race she leapt over a fence to congratulate him, revealing her body in the process. While her familial links with a series of great Olympic victors saved her from the death penalty set down for such a transgression, in future all trainers were required to appear naked to stop such a deception occurring again (Pausanias 5.6.7).

The gymnasium and Greek identity

As we saw above, for Pausanias the gymnasium was one of the crucial structures that any Greek city ought to possess (10.4.1). The association of the gymnasium with Hellenic identity seems to have become particularly important during the Hellenistic period, when the Greek world expanded as a result of the conquests of Alexander the Great and the new kingdoms formed by his successors. During this period attendance at the gymnasium became an important sign of an adherence to Greek culture, even for groups whose cultural heritage was very different. During the reign of the Seleukid king Antiochos IV in the first half of the second century BC, a group of pro-Greek Jews decided to adopt certain features of Greek life. One of their most important acts was to build a gymnasium in Jerusalem, an act fiercely attacked by the hard-line Jewish opinion reflected in I and II Maccabees (e.g. I Maccabees 1.10-25 = Austin 168).

In Egypt too membership of the gymnasium became a sign of Greek identity and status, helping to divide off the educated Greek classes from the rest of Egyptian society. Much of our archaeological evidence comes from precisely this period, when gymnasia began to be built throughout the cities of the eastern Mediterranean. Inscriptions also provide evidence for people from traditionally non-Greek communities taking part in Greek festivals, such as the Sidonian who is praised on an inscription for having won the chariot race at Nemea around 200 BC (Austin 121).

Chapter 11

The Gymnasium and Education

As we have seen, certain gymnasia could be specifically set aside for boys or youths and were used as places for both physical and mental training. The gymnasium or palaestra seems always to have played an important part in education, as evidenced by the description of the 'old-style' education in Aristophanes' *Clouds*. Here the supporter of traditional education, opposing the new forms of education introduced by the Sophists, looks back nostalgically to a time when boys sat naked and obediently in the gymnasium (960-1063). His memory is tinged with a voyeuristic delight in the imprints of these naked bodies, showing the link with erotics which we will discuss further below.

Ancient education involved three main areas – physical training, carried out by the *paidotribes* in the palaestra, training in letters (reading, writing and memorising) by the *didaskalos* and musical training. Education was a private matter, paid for by individuals for their sons, rather than being funded by the state, so the amount of education any boy received would depend on his family's wealth. In the Hellenistic period this changed with the institution of schools by wealthy benefactors which were designed to be open to all free children (inscriptions tell us of examples at Miletos and Teos in Asia Minor, *Syll.* 577, 578 = Austin 119, 120), though attendance would still have relied upon a boy being free from the duty of labouring for his family. In general, then, anything more than a basic education was restricted to the wealthier members of society.

Physical training in the gymnasium had two main aspects, which may sometimes have conflicted with one another. On the one hand was the role of physical education as part of a balanced education of both mind and body. This is the ideal proclaimed by many of the philosophers. Plato divided education into two main areas – gymnic, concerning the body, and musical, concerning the soul (*Laws* 795d). Aristotle expands these by suggesting that there are four main areas of education – reading and writing, physical exercises, music and drawing, and he stipulates that education of the body should precede education of the mind (*Politics* 1337b-38b). However, physical training in the gymnasium could also lead to more formal competition in athletic festivals. Reviews of progress often took the form of festival competitions, with miniature festivals held in the gymnasium. The Miletos decree also stipulates that the athletic trainers should be allowed to take athletes to perform at sacred games, and it is likely that promising candidates were identified during their education in the gymnasium. However, the training of youths for specific competition could also be criticised, especially by the philosophers. Aristotle is adamant that training in athletics should not overtake other forms of education and warns that over-specialised training, involving special diets and heavy exercises, could actually be harmful to very young athletes (*Politics* 1339a)

The exercises of the gymnasium

Evidence for the events which took place in the gymnasium comes from a variety of sources. In addition to the evidence to be gleaned from literary sources, such as the detailed prescriptions given in Philostratos' *Gymnastikos*, much of our information comes from the scenes of the gymnasium which decorated Athenian pottery, or from statues or statuettes.

Exercise in the gymnasium began with preparation of the athlete's body. The skin was rubbed with oil, probably to help protect it. After

15. Vase painting showing an athlete bathing. Behind him an aryballos and strigil hang on the wall.

exercise this oil, along with accumulated dirt and sweat, was then scraped off with a curved blade, the *strigil*. Representations of athletes often show then carrying an oil flask (*aryballos*) and strigil, or show these objects hanging on the wall of the gymnasium (Fig. 15). Roman writers also refer to dust or powder which was applied to the athlete's body, possibly to help provide a grip during wrestling, or else after exercising to condition the skin or for aesthetic reasons (Philostratos, *Gymnastikos* 56 = *Arete* 19).

Athletic exercises were divided into two groups, light and heavy. Heavy athletics consisted of the combat sports of wrestling, boxing and the pancration (a form of all-in-wrestling). These could take place in the open air, in the centre of the palaestra, and punch-bags were also set up in rooms in the gymnasium for boxers to practise with. Boxers also wore gloves. Originally these were leather thongs wrapped around the hands to protect them and give added strength to the wrist. In the fourth century BC more substantial gloves were introduced which ran up the arm and were reinforced with a knuckle guard (as on Fig. 13). These could cause substantial damage to opponents, and were probably only used in competition rather than in training within the gymnasium. In the Roman period some boxers are shown wearing spiked gloves, which must have inflicted even nastier injuries (Fig. 16). Indeed, boxing was a vicious sport, and a number of satirical epigrams talk of athletes who were so badly injured as to be unrecognisable, even to their wives or pet dogs! Boxing and pancration matches seem to have only come to an end when one of the

16. Scene of boxers wearing spiked boxing gloves on a mosaic at Ostia.

17. Vase painting showing an athlete holding jumping weights during the long jump.

contestants admitted defeat, whereas in wrestling it was the athlete who had thrown his opponent to the ground three times who was named victorious.

Light exercises consisted of what we would now term athletics – running, the long-jump, throwing the discus, and throwing the javelin. These four contexts, with the addition of wrestling, made up the pentathlon, and for many this was the best form of athletics since it produced a well-rounded physique (e.g. Aristotle, *Rhetoric* 1361b = *Arete* 48) The precise details of these events have been reconstructed through visual and literary evidence. Thus we know that unlike modern athletes, in the ancient long-jump the athletes used jumping weights (*halteres*) to help propel them through the air (Fig. 17). Some confusions still remain, however. The record jump of 55 feet attributed to the athlete Phayllos of Kroton has led many to suppose that it was a triple jump, but in the absence of any other secure evidence for this it might be safer to conclude that the number is due to exaggeration. Vase evidence has shown that the javelin was thrown with the aid of a leather thong wrapped around the shaft, as well as revealing the positions adopted in the throwing of the discus. It seems that distance of throw was the main criterion governing success, though some have argued that accuracy might also have been an issue. The way that the pentathlon was judged still remains obscure, though it appears that an athlete had to win three of the five contests to become the winner.

Military training in the gymnasium

After a general physical education, older youths seem to have undergone training in the skills necessary for warfare. This becomes particularly clear from the fourth century BC onwards with the formal institution of the *ephebeia* at Athens, although the Spartan education system had always been associated with training for war and some have suggested that the development of the gymnasium in the sixth century was due to the rising need for formal physical training to prepare for hoplite warfare. Aristotle describes the *ephebeia* at Athens, as practised in the mid-fourth century BC (*Athenian Constitution* 42). This was a period of two years' training given to every male citizen between the ages of 18 and 20 (youths of this age were known as ephebes). It involved training in weapons such as javelin-throwing and archery, as well as the youths acting as garrisons for forts on the outskirts of Attica. Only at the end of this two-year service could a youth become a full citizen of Athens. This link between the *ephebeia* and citizenship was important elsewhere too, and endured into the Roman period. Pausanias tells us that no one could be enrolled as a citizen at Pellene in Achaia unless he had first served as an ephebe (Pausanias 7.27.5).

The Beroia inscription

An inscription found at Beroia in Macedonia and dating to the early second century BC helps to give an idea of the regulations affecting the gymnasium and the sorts of activities that took place here (*SEG* 27.261 = *Arete* 185, Austin 118). It sets out rules concerning the appointment of those in charge of the gymnasium and the ways in which the establishment is to be run. Different regulations apply to the different age-groups – those under 30, the ephebes and those under 22 (probably all aged between 18 and 22) and the boys (*paides*), presumably those under 18. Contact between the different groups is discouraged and certain groups of people are excluded from exercising in the gymnasium altogether, including slaves and freedmen, a comment which shows that this is an institution strictly limited to free-born citizens, though some of the trainers could be slaves. The ephebes are to train in javelin-throwing and archery – pursuits with a clear military link. The progress of the boys is to be examined by reviews three times a year, while the achievements of all those exercising is also put to the test at the *Hermaia* festival, held annually. This festival is a miniature version of those held at a civic level and includes sacrifices to Hermes, the god of the gymnasium, and a banquet, as well as various contests. For the young men up to the age of 30 contests are set in fitness, good discipline and hard training, where the victor is rewarded with the prize of a weapon. There is a clear sense here of the link between training in the gymnasium and preparation for warfare. A torch race is also held for the boys and youths, a contest that is often held as part of ephebic festivals. These festivals often seem to have a great concentration on team games, presumably because of the skills of working together that these helped to develop and the potential usefulness of such skills in warfare. The skills tested in the gymnasium at Beroia are also developed in other Hellenistic ephebic training. Inscriptions from Athens in particular recall the good discipline shown by the ephebes during the various public festivals and processions in which they took part.

Erotics in the gymnasium

As a place where men of different ages could gather together, even if this was sometimes constrained by law, the gymnasium was also a place where homosexual friendships and relationships could develop. The dialogues of Plato give us an idea of the ideal form of such relationships in ancient Athens. It was a friendship where a young man, the *erastes* or lover, would select a younger boy, his *eromenos*, beloved, in order to educate him in politics and philosophy as well as to enjoy a sexual relationship. Many of the Platonic dialogues show how this relationship might form in the confines of the gymnasium. In the *Lysis*, Sokrates enters a palaestra where a young man Hippothales has been struck by the beauty of the young Lysis. Vase paintings showing gymnasium scenes often also show scenes of homosexual courtship between bearded men and younger boys (Fig. 18, overleaf). The beautiful naked bodies of athletes in the gymnasium often seem to have invited an erotic response from those viewing them. One of the features praised in a beloved was a sense of youthful modesty and reserve. This comes over particularly clearly in statuary too, where the victorious athlete is often shown looking down at the ground, avoiding our gaze.

18. The decoration of this red-figure kylix links together athletic scenes on the exterior with homosexual courtship in the interior.

Chapter 12

The Structures

Our knowledge of the structures which made up the gymnasium becomes much clearer in the Hellenistic period, when a number of the surviving archaeological examples were first built. The earliest is the gymnasium at Delphi which first dates to around 334/3 BC, with further additions in the second half of the third century BC (Fig. 19). It includes a running track

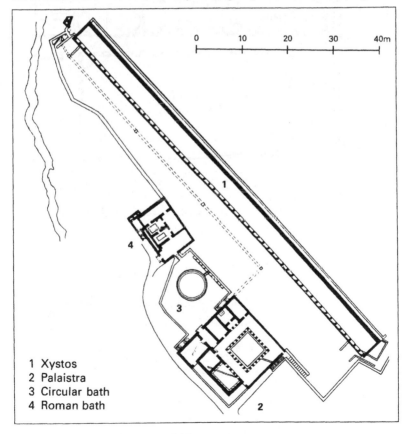

1 Xystos
2 Palaistra
3 Circular bath
4 Roman bath

19. Plan of the gymnasium at Delphi.

(*xystos*) on the higher level and below this the palaestra – a courtyard surrounded by a portico with rooms off it on two sides. Next to the palaestra is a circular bath for the athletes to bathe in. Another bath complex was added later, in the Roman period. A similar complex including both a palaestra and running tracks can be found at Olympia, and seems to date from the third century BC. Here a Doric colonnade forms a peristyle with rooms opening off it while running tracks were later added to the north (see Fig. 6).

An account of the layout of the Greek palaestra by the Roman writer and architect Vitruvius (*On Architecture* 5.11 = *Arete* 179) names the rooms which it contained. In addition to a central *exedra* which could

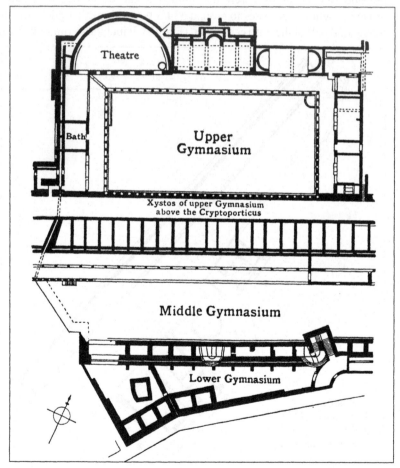

20. Plan of the gymnasium at Pergamon.

serve as the *ephebeion* – the classroom for the ephebes – Vitruvius names the *coryceum* (punch-bag room, *korykeion* in Greek), the *conisterium* (*konisterion*, literally 'dust' room, probably where the sand was kept or the dust which athletes rubbed over their bodies) as well as the *loutron* (bath) and *elaeosthesium*, a place for the athletes to oil themselves. Surviving examples of palaestrai, such as those at Delphi and Olympia, show the combination of open and closed rooms opening off the porticoes of the palaestra. The open ones are *exedrai*, places for meeting and conversations (like those mentioned in Plato's dialogues) while the smaller closed rooms could serve as the other rooms identified by Vitruvius.

Many of the best preserved gymnasia, however, come from the eastern Mediterranean and were set up by cities rather than sanctuaries. The largest preserved example comes from the Attalid kingdom of Pergamon, a powerful and prestigious city during the Hellenistic period (Fig. 20). The gymnasium is built on three levels on the south-eastern slope of the Acropolis, in the area of the city which was extended by the King Eumenes II (reigned 197-158 BC). It dates to the first half of the second century BC, but received numerous additions during the course of time, not least in the Roman imperial period when baths and an auditorium/theatre were added to the upper level. Inscriptions found in the complex call it the gymnasium

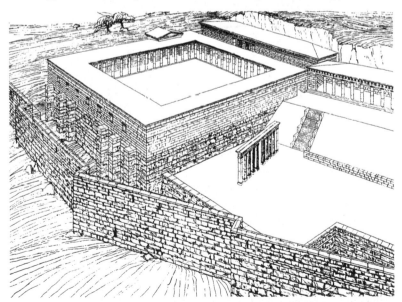

21. Reconstruction of the lower gymnasium at Priene, with the adjoining stadium.

22. Drawing of the graffiti found in the ephebeion of the gymnasium at Priene.

of the youths (*neoi*), but it also seems to have served as the training ground for the ephebes of the city.

The educational use of the gymnasium by a city's ephebes is perhaps most vividly shown in the lower gymnasium at Priene, a city further down the western coast of Asia Minor. Here the gymnasium occupies an open area below the main body of the city, and adjoins the stadium, which could have been used for exercise and training when it was not being used for festival competitions (Fig. 21). It was built in the second half of the second century BC. Access to the complex is from the west. The northern side of the palaestra is set back from the open courtyard by a double colonnade. In the north-western corner lies the *loutron*, complete with lions' head water spouts and basins for washing. In the centre is a large open exedra which clearly served as the city's *ephebeion*. The walls of this room are covered with graffiti written by the pupils, who stake their claim to a space by writing their names, e.g. 'the place of Alexander' (*ho topos Alexandrou*), the ancient equivalent of 'Alex was here' (Fig. 22).

Chapter 13

The Greek Gymnasium in the Roman World

The gymnasium did not lose its importance when the cities of the Greek east came under the power of the Roman Empire. Pausanias' account of his experiences of Greece in the second century AD shows the enduring importance of the gymnasium as a critical amenity for any Greek city to possess (10.4.1) and the *ephebeia*'s place in civic education (7.27.5). The close ties between Greek cities and their gymnasia were also well-known to the Romans, as is shown by a letter of the emperor Trajan, written to Pliny the Younger when he was acting as his representative in the province of Bithynia. Pliny had consulted Trajan over the plans of the Nicaeans to rebuild their gymnasium. Trajan's reply is to suggest that they may have been over-ambitious in their plans, commenting (rather patronisingly) that 'these little Greeks love their gymnasia' (Pliny, *Letters* 10.40). Indeed, a number of new gymnasia were built throughout the Hellenistic and Roman periods. In the Roman period, they were usually combined with a Roman-style bathing complex. Some of the clearest examples come from Ephesos, the centre of the Roman province of Asia. Here a number of bath-gymnasium complexes were built during the first and second centuries AD, mostly funded by wealthy benefactors. All combine areas for athletic activity with a series of rooms for bathing (Fig. 23). The educational aspect of the gymnasium could also be included within its plan and decoration. The East Bath-gymnasium at Ephesos included a room with tiered benches off its palaestra, probably to be used as a lecture room, while an auditorium was added to the Hellenistic gymnasium at Pergamon. The Baths of Faustina in Miletos, constructed in the mid-second century AD, also alluded to the educational side of the gymnasium through their sculptural decoration. A room at the end of the main entrance hall was filled with statues of the nine Muses, as well as with portraits of the imperial couple, Marcus Aurelius and Faustina.

Indeed, the more formal educational side of the gymnasium also continued into the Roman period with the survival of the *ephebeia*. Numerous inscriptions attest to the victories of ephebes in local festivals in their home towns, and they also played an important part in civic religious life, participating in public processions. In Sparta the educational

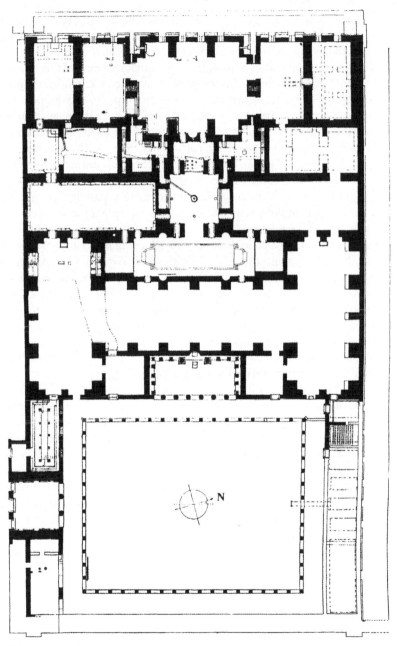

23. Plan of the Baths of Vedius at Ephesos showing its division between bathing rooms (to the west) and the gymnasium area (to the east).

system attracted particular attention. Sparta had always been renowned for the harshness of its military training, and in the Roman period the city seems to have made a deliberate attempt to revive that training as a sign of its traditional qualities. One of the most famous aspects of this training was the 'Whipping contest', a competition at which the youths of Sparta would line up in front of the Altar of Artemis Orthia to be whipped. The aim was to endure the pain as long as possible, with the result that the contest also became known as the endurance test (*agon tes karterias*). Roman writers seem to have been particularly enthralled by this re-enactment of traditional Spartan endurance and the contest attracted numerous spectators. Indeed, some writers claimed that youths would go as far as dying rather than give in, a test of endurance that has parallels in a number of stories about athletic heroes too. The best example is the sixth-century BC pancratiast Arrachion of Phigalia who was proclaimed victor at Olympia even though he died in the course of achieving his victory. The story is told by both Pausanias (8.40.1-2) and Philostratos (who calls him Arrichion, *Gymnastikos* 21; *Imagines* 2.7.5). While competing in the pancration Arrachion managed to dislocate his opponent's ankle just as he himself was being strangled. The pain caused his opponent to admit defeat at the very moment that Arrachion died, leading the judges to award the victory to his corpse. While few if any boys probably did die during the Spartan endurance contest, the idea that their love of glory might lead them to consider death better than dishonour still packed a powerful ideological punch.

Ephebic training also continued in other cities during the Roman period, though it was probably limited to the sons of the local aristocracy, whose names are often recorded on stelai set up to record the ephebes for a particular year. A number of these stelai have been found in Athens, showing that the *ephebeia* here continued well into the third century AD. Some of them are decorated with reliefs showing the contests in which the boys competed. The *naumachia*, or naval contest, is particularly prominent, and probably alludes to the contests in which ephebes took part during festivals celebrating Athens' naval victory over the Persians at Salamis back in 480 BC (Fig. 24). Memory of their achievements during the Classical past was an important source of prestige for the Greek cities of the Roman Empire, and these reliefs suggest that Athenian youths helped to re-enact that past glory through their ephebic contests.

The Roman response to the gymnasium

The traditional picture of the Roman attitude to Greek athletics is one of disdain. Indeed, the Greek practice of exercising naked could be viewed

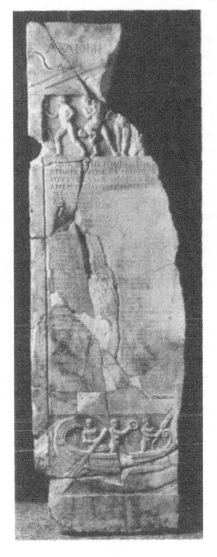

24. Athenian ephebic relief dating to AD 192/3, with a scene of a naval contest at the base and the torch race and pancration at the top.

with suspicion as likely to lead to effeminacy and pederasty. Cicero quotes with approval Ennius' declaration that 'to strip the body naked among citizens is the fount of shame' (*Tusculan Disputations* 4.70), in the course of a discussion of the origin of pederastic relations in the gymnasium. The Romans were also hostile to the idea of public performance in athletic competitions. Indeed, for Cornelius Nepos this was a key difference between the Greeks and Romans:

Almost everywhere in Greece, it was held to be a great honour to be proclaimed victor at Olympia ... but among us all these things [acting and athletics] are regarded as disgraceful or lowly and quite removed from honourable behaviour. (Cornelius Nepos, *preface* 5)

While some Romans did take part in contests such as the chariot-racing at Olympia, few seem to have won significant success in athletic contests, and indeed among the victors at the Capitoline Games in Rome we know of no athletic victors from Rome or Italy even though a number of Romans won success in the poetic contests. Thus far, the traditional picture seems to be close to the truth.

However, while few Romans seem to have taken part in public athletic festivals, they did eagerly embrace the physical culture of the Greek gymnasium. During the first century AD we hear with increasing frequency of Roman citizens indulging in Greek-style exercises within the baths of Rome. Juvenal's third satire is a tirade about the extent to which Roman culture has become tainted by foreign influences, and athletics draws his fire as much as anything. So he complains about the rustic Roman who wears prizes of victory on his oiled neck, or the crafty Greek who can take on the role of personal trainer as easily as that of doctor or rhetorician (*Satire* 3.68, 72). Martial too records the tendencies of bathers to exercise with weights and by wrestling in the baths, while Pliny the Younger laments the fact that people no longer train under the eye of a Roman military veteran but choose instead to be coached by a Greek trainer ('Graeculus magister', *Panegyric* 13.5).

The archaeological evidence paints a similar picture. During the course of the first three centuries AD a number of public bath complexes were built which included areas for physical exercise as well as rooms for bathing. In connection with his founding of the *Neronia* festival in AD 60, the emperor Nero is said to have constructed baths and a gymnasium on the Campus Martius in Rome, and to have provided free oil to the senatorial and equestrian classes when these were opened, suggesting that he was trying to promote an adoption of the Greek gymnasium lifestyle among the Roman upper classes (Suetonius, *Nero* 12.3). The decoration of bath complexes could also refer to the gymnasium through athletic images. Lysippos' bronze Apoxyomenos statue of an athlete scraping the oil off his body with a strigil had been set up outside Agrippa's baths while later bath complexes often included replicas of famous Greek athletic statues such as Myron's Diskobolos.

Yet as well as recalling the athletes of the Classical past, the decoration could also allude to contemporary sporting heroes. Excavations at Ostia have revealed a number of mosaics with scenes of sporting activity, placed within bath complexes (e.g. Fig. 16), while the Baths of Caracalla at Rome, built in the first half of the third century AD, were decorated with coloured mosaics showing a series of victorious athletes. Sometimes individual athletes were even named on mosaics, as in an inn at Ostia which shows a pancration contest between two famous athletes of the early third century AD, Aurelius Alexander and Aurelius Helix (Fig. 25). These images show the popularity of contemporary athletic festivals in the Roman world. The appearance of similar images in bath complexes also suggests that Roman bathers liked to make a connection between their own exercises and the athletic prowess of these sporting heroes, creating a fantasy world in which they could see their own activities as comparable.

25. Mosaic celebrating the athletes Alexander and Helix in an inn at Ostia.

Chapter 14

Athletics and Warfare

Roman writers keenly rejected the notion that athletics might form a useful training for warfare. In Lucan's *Civil War*, Caesar urges on his troops by telling them that they will encounter only the youth of Greece, which has been so weakened by its time in the gymnasium and palaestra that it can scarcely bear arms (*Civil War* 7.270-2). Greek writers too could criticise the idea that athletics formed a useful training for warfare. In a fragment of Euripides' *Autolykos*, mentioned above (pp. 50-1), the speaker angrily asks

> What man has ever defended the city of his ancestors by wrestling well, by being fleet-footed, or by winning a crown for throwing the discus or hitting his opponent on the chin? Do men fight their enemies with discuses in their hands or throw them from their land by using their hands to punch through shields? No one is so stupid when he is standing in front of a weapon. (Euripides, *Autolykos* fragment 282.16-23 = *Arete* 230)

Lucian's *Anacharsis*, written in the second century AD, also plays with the two sides of the question. The piece is an imaginary dialogue between the Athenian law-giver Solon and the Skythian sage Anacharsis, set in sixth-century Athens in the Lyceum gymnasium. Anacharsis expresses amazement at the athletic activities which he sees taking place before him, while Solon attempts to defend these as playing an important part in the education of citizen youths. In particular, this education is said to help youths prepare for their role as the defenders of the city and to train men for warfare. It gives them a stamina which is set in powerful contrast to the weak, pale bodies of those who have not trained in this way and therefore wilt in battle under the heat of the sun. Solon is keen to stress the usefulness of all athletic pursuits as a training for warfare. Jumping practice helps when one needs to jump over ditches, training in throwing the javelin and the discus have a direct military link, and wrestling while covered in mud helps prepare one for the need to carry the body of a wounded friend off the battlefield (27-8). Lucian seems to exaggerate these arguments for comic effect, and indeed Anacharsis remains unconvinced, pointing out that naked bodies arc no defence against weapons and dismissing athletic exercises as childish amusements. Both Solon's and Anacharsis' arguments have resonances elsewhere in ancient literature. In Plutarch's biography of Philopoemen athletic training is contrasted with military training:

> The athletic body and training are different in every way from the military and the diet and exercise are especially different, since athletes are always strengthening themselves with a lot of sleep and perpetual stuffing of their stomachs ... the soldier on the other hand has to be experienced in every sort of wandering and irregularity, and especially able to bear easily lack of food and sleeplessness. (Plutarch, *Philopoemen*, 3)

Yet these attacks often relate specifically to over-specialisation in athletic training as opposed to a moderate athletic training such as that practised in the gymnasium. And despite the criticisms, the link between sport and warfare remained pervasive throughout Greek thought. We have already seen that the gymnasium was the training ground both for athletes and warriors, and that Homer's warriors indulge in athletics in their spare time. At Olympia too the contests in the stadium and the monuments commemorating them were set side by side with monuments recalling the victories of various states in military campaigns.

Successful athletes were also often presented as helping to save their cities in times of warfare. Diodorus Sikylos records how the Olympic victor Milon was said to have won victory for the city of Kroton, despite their enemy outnumbering them three to one (12.9.5-6). Pausanias records a similar story about Oibotas of Dyme being present at the battle of Plataia (in 479 BC) though he rejects it on the grounds that Oibotas won his victories in the sixth Olympic festival, in 756 BC! Another crown victor who was said to have taken part in an important Panhellenic victory was the three-times Pythian victor Phayllos of Croton, who brought a ship to help the Greeks in the Battle of Salamis (Herodotus 8.47).

These stories about the involvement of athletic victors in important battles suggest that victories at crown festivals could give athletes an almost superhuman aura, enabling them to achieve great feats in warfare too. Even in the Roman period successful athletes could also be recalled for their military achievements, as we see in Pausanias' account of the runner Mnesiboulos of Elateia. After winning numerous prizes for running this man died defending his home city from the raids of the Kostobokoi in the late second century AD (Pausanias 10.34.5).

Chapter 15

Women and Athletics

Women have not had much of a place in this account and, in general, athletics does seem to have been a male-dominated activity in the ancient world. Married women were banned from attending the contests at Olympia, though they could still compete *in absentia* in the equestrian contests, like Kyniska of Sparta. However, there were some festivals in which women could take part in athletic contests. At Olympia a festival in honour of Hera was held which included running races for girls, divided into age categories in a manner similar to that of the male contests (Pausanias 5.16.2-7 = *Arete* 158). There is even some scattered evidence for women competing at other Panhellenic sites. An inscription found at Delphi records the victories of three sisters, the daughters of Hermesianax of Tralles in Asia Minor, who won victories in the stade races at Delphi, Isthmia and Nemea (*Syll.* 802 = *Arete* 162). It is unclear from this whether the girls competed in mixed races, or female-only events. The inscription dates to AD 47 and it is possible that the introduction of women to these festivals was a Roman development.

However, we do also have earlier evidence for women exercising outside the festival sphere as part of education or religious ritual. This is clearest at Sparta where we hear that the famous lawgiver Lykourgos prescribed exercises and contests for girls as well as for boys so that they should develop strong bodies, fit for producing strong children (Xenophon, *Constitution of the Lakedaimonians* 1.4 = *Arete* 152; see also Plutarch, *Lykourgos* 14.2-15.1 = *Arete* 153). Mixed exercising could be attacked by some as leading to immorality – a view we find expressed in Euripides' *Andromache* (595-601) where the immodest exercises of Spartan girls are blamed as leading to a lack of chastity. Yet there is also evidence for female athletics elsewhere in Greece. The sanctuary of Artemis at Brauron in Attica has yielded a number of vases showing young girls running, and it is thought that here races formed part of the initiation rituals in this female-only cult. Until recent years little research had been done on women's athletics. As with other areas of research into ancient athletics, it is likely that here too the picture will change significantly as new evidence is uncovered and old sources re-examined.

Chapter 16

Conclusions

The culture of ancient Greece was a fiercely competitive one. Wars between neighbouring cities were frequent, passionate debates took place in the assembly and law courts, and even in the theatre rival playwrights were battling to outdo one another. Athletics played a key role in this agonistic culture. Sport provided yet another stage on which men and cities could struggle for supremacy, and victories here were celebrated just as greatly as those in politics or war. Indeed, as we have seen, athletics could provide a training for war, and also take its place, as an alternative battleground on which civic rivalries were played out.

Athletics was also closely linked to education, and gymnasia served as schools and military academies as well as providing leisure facilities for other adult male citizens. The culture of physical beauty that developed in the gymnasium also had an influence on art, expressed in the plentiful athletic scenes on vase paintings as well as in both lost and surviving statues in marble and bronze. The need to celebrate victories at the Panhellenic festivals led not only to the development of victory statues but also to a new literary genre, the epinician ode, whose paeans of praise have survived the centuries just as Pindar promised. Yet not everyone agreed with the exaltation of athletic heroes – intellectuals could lament the stress put on physical rather than mental prowess, while others were concerned about over-specialisation or unhealthy training regimes.

The continuation and development of athletic competitions and the gymnasium through the Hellenistic and Roman periods, and the frequent references to athletic activity in texts and inscriptions, also offer us insights into its enduring importance as a symbol of Greek culture, and the ways that culture adapted itself to changing historical circumstances. Much work still remains to be done, especially on these later periods, and also into the relatively unstudied area of women's athletics. As well as increasing our understanding of ancient sport, the study of ancient athletics can also provide an insight into the world of Greek culture and society as a whole, helping us to understand both the similarities and the great differences between the ancient world and our own.

Chronological Periods and Some Important Dates

Archaic: mid-8th century to 480 BC

776 BC	Traditional foundation date for the Olympic Games
mid-8th cent. BC	Homer's *Iliad* and *Odyssey*
720 BC	Olympic Victory of Orsippos of Megara, traditional date for introduction of athletic nudity
586 BC	Start of Pythian Games at Delphi
582 BC	Start of Isthmian Games
573 BC	Start of Nemean Games
566 BC	Start of Great Panathenaia festival at Athens
mid-6th cent. BC	Earliest references to gymnasium
	Earliest examples of epinician poetry (Ibykos)
540-516 BC	Victories of Milon of Kroton
490-473 BC	Victories of Theagenes of Thasos
488-480 BC	Victories of Astylos of Kroton (later Syracuse)
480 BC	Battle of Salamis again Persians
c. 480 BC	Victories of Phayllus of Kroton

Classical: 480 to 323 BC (Death of Alexander the Great)

c. 496-446 BC	Pindar's epinician odes
c. 470-457 BC	Construction of the Temple of Zeus at Olympia
400 BC	Hippias of Elis composes list of Olympic victors
396 BC	Victory of Kyniska of Sparta

Hellenistic: 323 to 31 BC (Battle of Actium)

c. 280 BC	Introduction of Ptolemeia festival at Alexandria
from 221/0 BC	Festival of Artemis Leukophryene instituted at Magnesia on the Maeander
c. 200 BC	Foundation of school at Miletos
2nd cent. BC	Foundation of school at Teos
c. 200-150 BC	Beroia inscription
c. 175-167 BC	Building of Gymnasium at Jerusalem
146 BC	Mainland Greece becomes Roman province

133 BC   Pergamene kingdom in Asia Minor inherited by
                 Rome

Roman Imperial: 31 BC to 4th century AD
30/28 BC   Augustus institutes Actian festival at Nikopolis in
                 Greece
2 BC/AD 2   Sebasta festival at Naples
AD 60   Nero institutes Neronia in Rome
AD 66-7   Nero competes at festivals in Greece
AD 86   Domitian institutes Capitoline Games at Rome
mid-2nd cent. AD Guild of athletic victors set up headquarters at Rome
AD 160-180   Pausanias writing his *Guide to Greece*
AD 220s   Philostratus writing the *Gymnastikos*
AD 385   Latest attested Olympic victor
AD 393 or 426   Possible dates for last ancient Olympic Games
                            *
AD 1896   First modern Olympic Games held at Athens (earlier
                 revivals in Greece from 1859)

Suggestions for Further Study

- How have the ancient Olympics been used in the service of modern ideologies since the introduction of modern Olympic games in the nineteenth century?
- What roles did the ancient gymnasium play?
- How important were festivals in ancient Greek society?
- How 'democratic' was ancient sport?
- What evidence is there for the origins of sporting activity in either religious worship or initiation ritual?
- Can we use athletic activity as an index of Greekness?
- Compare Pindar's *Victory Odes* and the surviving evidence of Greek athletic statues. Do they celebrate the same sorts of qualities? What overlaps or differences are there between the portrayal of athletes in art and literature?
- How much did Greek athletics change from Archaic Greece to Late Antiquity?
- What links existed between athletics and warfare?

Further Reading

I have generally kept to works in English here, though a couple of the more crucial works in other languages are noted in passing.

Glossary
M. Golden, *Sport in the Ancient World from A to Z* (London and New York, 2004).
There is also a useful glossary in the back of S.G. Miller, *Ancient Greek Athletics* (New Haven and London, 2004).

Collections of source material
S.G. Miller, *Arete: Greek Sports from Ancient Sources* (3rd expanded edn, Berkeley, Los Angeles and London, 2004) – includes epigraphical as well as literary evidence.
W.E. Sweet, *Sport and Recreation in Ancient Greece* (Oxford and New York, 1987), includes some visual evidence as well as literary and epigraphic texts.
R.S. Robinson, *Sources for the History of Greek Athletics in English Translation* (Cincinnati, 1955) is less useful.

The crucial works on athletic inscriptions are in French and Italian. Louis Robert's articles are scattered in numerous journals, but a number are collected in his *Opera Minora Selecta*. Luigi Moretti collected a number of inscriptions relating to festivals and athletic victors in L. Moretti, *Iscrizioni agonistiche greche* (Rome, 1953) as well as the names of Olympic victors in L. Moretti, *Olympionikai: i vincitori negli antichi agoni olimpici* (*Atti della Accademia Nazionale dei Lincei* 8; Rome, 1957), with two supplements in *Klio* 52 (1970), 295-303 and *Miscellanea Greca e Romana* 12 (1987), 67-91.

Exhibition catalogues published on the occasion of various modern Olympic Games often contain useful essays and examples of the art and architecture relating to athletics. In particular, see *Mind and Body. Athletic Contests in Ancient Greece* (Hellenic Ministry of Culture, Athens, 1989) and T. Measham, E. Spathar and P. Donnelly (eds) *1000 Years of the*

Olympic Games: Treasures of Ancient Greece (Sydney 2000).

General accounts of athletics (most recent first)

S.G. Miller, *Ancient Greek Athletics* (New Haven and London, 2004). This is set to become the new textbook on Greek athletics. It is lavishly illustrated and provides a detailed account of individual contests and the practicalities of festivals.

N. Spivey, *The Ancient Olympics* (Oxford, 2004). A good general account of how athletics fitted into Greek society and particularly on its connections with warfare.

W.B. Tyrrell, *The Smell of Sweat: Greek Athletics, Olympics and Culture* (Wauconda, Il, 2004). A general account of festivals and contests, comes with CD of source materials.

T.F. Scanlon, *Eros and Greek Athletics* (Oxford, 2002) is particularly concerned with the erotic associations of athletic activity. This is especially good on the evidence for female athletics.

M. Golden, *Sport and Society in Ancient Greece* (Cambridge, 1998). An excellent account of how athletics worked within Greek society, particularly in the creation of distinctions between different groups.

M.B. Poliakoff, *Combat Sports in the Ancient World: Competition, Violence and Culture* (New Haven and London, 1987). Discusses the details of individual contests and the role of violence in ancient society.

D. Sansone, *Greek Athletics and the Genesis of Sport* (Berkeley, Los Angeles and London, 1988). A provocative account which reads sport as the symbolic sacrifice of energy in honour of the gods – not accepted by all!

Collections of articles

N.B. Crowther, *Athletika: Studies on the Olympic Games and Greek Athletics* (Nikephoros Beiheftei 11; Hildesheim, 2004) is a collection of the author's many articles on Greek athletics, with useful updates of the recent scholarship.

D.J. Phillips and D. Pritchard (eds), *Sport and Festival in the Ancient Greece World* (Swansea, 2003) is a collection of essays on different aspects of the Olympics and other festivals in Antiquity.

W.J. Raschke (ed.), *The Archaeology of the Olympics* (Madison, Wisconsin, 1988) contains lots of useful articles summarising recent research, much of which is otherwise not published in English. See especially Mallwitz on the early history of Olympia, and Glass on gymnasia.

Older accounts
Some of the interpretations offered in these are now rather out-dated, but
they still contain much useful information, particularly on the details of
individual events:
E.N. Gardiner, *Greek Athletic Sports and Festivals* (London, 1910).
―――, *Athletics of the Ancient World* (London, 1930).
H.A. Harris, *Greek Athletes and Athletics* (London, 1964).
―――, *Sport in Greece and Rome* (London, 1972).

The Olympic Games
All of the above discuss the Olympics, but for specific accounts see:
J. Swaddling, *The Ancient Olympic Games* (3rd edn, London, 2004) which
    also provides much general information about training and the individ-
    ual events.
U. Sinn, *Olympia: Cult, Sport and Ancient Festival* (English translation,
    Princeton, 2000) which gives a good account of the archaeological
    remains.
M.I. Finley and H.W. Pleket, *The Olympic Games: The First Thousand
    Years* (London, 1976) also gives a useful overview.

For lists of victors and their origins see:
T.F. Scanlon, *Eros and Greek Athletics* (Oxford, 2002), ch. 2.
N.B. Crowther, 'Elis and the Games' in *Antiquité Classique* 57 (1988),
    301-10 (also in his collected volume *Athletika*) concentrates on evi-
    dence for Elis' success in the Games.
A. Farrington, 'Olympic victors and the popularity of the Olympic Games
    in the Imperial period', *Tyche* 12 (1997), 15-46 gives a detailed account
    of the evidence, including its possible biases.

Regional accounts
D.G. Kyle, *Athletics in Ancient Athens* (Leiden, 1987) discusses the integra-
    tion of athletic culture in Athens in the Archaic and Classical periods.
N.M. Kennell, *The Gymnasium of Virtue: Education and Culture in
    Ancient Sparta* (Chapel Hill, 1995) discusses the Spartan educational
    system.

Festivals
L. Robert, 'Discours d'ouverture', *Praktika of the Eighth International
    Congress of Greek and Latin Epigraphy* (Athens, 1984), I. 35-45;
    reprinted in L. Robert, *Opera Minora Selecta* VI, 709-19 is the crucial
    account followed by many.

A.J.S. Spawforth, 'Agonistic festivals in Roman Greece' in S. Walker and A. Cameron (eds), *The Greek Renaissance in the Roman Empire* (*Bulletin of the Institute of Classical Studies* Supplement 55; London, 1989).

S. Mitchell, 'Festivals, games and civic life in Roman Asia Minor', *Journal of Roman Studies* 80 (1990), 183-93.

E.E. Rice, *The Grand Procession of Ptolemy Philadelphus* (Oxford, 1983) discusses the account of this procession in Athenaios and its connection to the *Ptolemeia* festival.

The social background of Athletes

Henri Pleket has done a great deal of work in this area. For accounts in English see H.W. Pleket, 'Games, prizes, athletes and ideology. Some aspects of the history of sport in the Greco-Roman world', *Stadion* (= *Arena*) 1 (1975), 49-89; id., 'The participants in the ancient Olympic games: social background and mentality', in W. Coulson and H. Kyrieleis (eds), *Proceedings of an International Symposium on the Olympic Games, 5-9 September 1988* (Athens, 1992); id., 'Sport and ideology in the Greco-Roman World', *Klio* 80 (1998), 315-24.

For accounts of athletes in the Roman period see O. van Nijf, 'Athletics, festivals and Greek identity in the Roman East', *Proceedings of the Cambridge Philological Society* 45 (1999), 176-200; reprinted in an expanded version as 'Local heroes: athletics, festivals and elite self-fashioning in the Roman East', in S. Goldhill (ed.), *Being Greek under Rome: Cultural Identity, the Second Sophistic and the Development of Empire* (Cambridge, 2001), and O. van Nijf, 'Inscriptions and civic memory in the Roman East', in A.E. Cooley (ed.), *The Afterlife of Inscriptions* (London, 2000) concentrating on the inscriptions from Termessos in Asia Minor.

Athletes and their cities, heroisation

J. Fontenrose, 'The hero as athlete', *California Studies in Classical Antiquity* 1 (1968), 73-104 gives an overview of the evidence.

J. Elsner, 'Image and ritual: reflections on the religious appreciation of Classical art', *Classical Quarterly* 46 (1996), 515-31 discusses the case of Theagenes of Thasos and his statue.

L. Kurke, 'The economy of kudos', in C. Dougherty and L. Kurke (eds), *Cultural Poetics in Archaic Greece: Cult, Performance, Politics* (Cambridge, 1993) explains these stories in the light of political and social pressures.

Pindar and Epinician odes

C.M. Bowra, *Pindar* (Oxford, 1964) is rather outdated but gives a general introduction. L. Kurke, *The Traffic in Praise: Pindar and the Poetics of Social Economy* (Ithaca and London, 1991) links the poems to their cultural context; see also P. O'Sullivan, 'Victory song, victory statue: Pindar's agonistic imagery and its legacy', in D.J. Phillips and D. Pritchard (eds), *Sport and Festival in the Ancient Greece World* (Swansea, 2003).

The Everyman text of Pindar – R. Stoneman (ed.), *Pindar. The Odes and Selected Fragments* (trans. G.S. Conway and R. Stoneman; London, 1997) – also provides a useful introduction.

The odes of Simonides, Ibykos and Bacchylides are translated in the Loeb edition of *Greek Lyric* vols 3 and 4 by D.A. Campbell.

Athletic statues

The standard account in English is still W.W. Hyde, *Olympic Victor Monuments and Greek Athletic Art* (Washington, 1921, reprinted University Press of Pacific, 2003), though see also W.J. Raschke, 'Images of victory: some new considerations of athletic monuments', in W.J. Raschke (ed.) *Archaeology of the Olympics: The Olympics and Other Festivals in Antiquity* (Madison, WI, 1988).

For those who read Italian, the best recent account is F. Rausa, *L'immagine del vincitore: L'atleta nella statuaria greca dell'età arcaica all' ellenismo* (Rome, 1994).

Nudity

J.A. Arieti, 'Nudity in Greek athletics', *Classical World* 68 (1974-5), 431-6; N.B. Crowther, 'Athletic dress and nudity in Greek athletics', *Eranos* 80 (1982), 163-8 (also in Crowther, *Athletika*) and M. MacDonnell, 'The introduction of athletic nudity: Thucydides, Plato and the vases', *Journal of Hellenic Studies* 111 (1991), 182-93 give accounts of the evidence and its interpretation.

On nudity in art see A. Stewart, *Art, Desire and the Body in Ancient Greece* (Cambridge, 1997), *passim* and L. Bonfante, 'Nudity as a costume in Classical art', *American Journal of Archaeology* 93 (1989), 543-70.

Athletics in the Roman period

J. König, *Athletics and Literature in the Roman Empire* (Cambridge, 2005) discusses the representation of athletics in literary and epigraphic texts during the Roman Empire.

Z. Newby, *Greek Athletics in the Roman World: Victory and Virtue*

(Oxford, 2005) focusses on the way that athletics was experienced in the Roman Empire through art.

Z. Newby, 'Greek athletics as Roman spectacle: the mosaics from Ostia and Rome', *Papers of the British School at Rome* 70 (2002), 177-203 looks at athletic scenes on mosaics in Italy.

The modern Olympics

David Young has written extensively about the foundation of the modern Olympics in 1896 and the values associated with them: D.C. Young, *The Olympic Myth of Greek Amateur Athletics* (Chicago, 1984); id., 'How the amateurs won the Olympics' in W.J. Raschke (ed.), *The Archaeology of the Olympics: The Olympics and Other Festivals in Antiquity* (Madison, WI, 1988) 55-75; id., *The Modern Olympics: A Struggle for Renewal* (Baltimore and London, 1996).

On the Berlin Olympics of 1936 see R.D. Mandell, *The Nazi Olympics* (London, 1971).

Other bibliographies of ancient sport

D.G. Kyle, 'Directions in ancient sport history', *Journal of Sport History* 10 (1983), 7-34.

T.F. Scanlon, *Greek and Roman Athletics: A Bibliography* (Chicago, 1984).

N.B. Crowther, 'Studies in Greek athletics', *Classical World* 78 (1984-5), 97-558 and 79 (1985-6), 73-135.

――――, 'Recent trends in the study of Greek athletics', *L'Antiquité Classique* 59 (1990), 246-55.

M. Golden, *Sport and Society in Ancient Greece* (Cambridge, 1998), 179-82.

Index

Greek Vases: An Introduction

Elizabeth Moignard

ISBN 1 85399 691 2

Greek Vases is an introduction to the painted vases which were an ever-present but understated feature of life in the Greek world between the end of the Bronze Age and the rise of Rome, and, in the modern world, an important component of museum collections since the eighteenth century. The book uses specific illustrated examples to explore the archaeological use of vases as chronological indicators, the use of the various shapes, their scenes of myth and everyday life and what these tell us, the way in which we think about their makers, and how they are treated today as museum objects and archaeological evidence.

Key features of the text include a brief, accessible introduction to the vases with school and university students in mind, discussion of the different approaches to vases adopted by their very different groups of users, and an approach designed to help viewers understand how to look at these fascinating objects for themselves.

The Plays of Sophocles

A.F. Garvie

ISBN 1 85399 680 7

The emphasis throughout this concise, informative and stimulating book is on Sophocles' tragic thinking, on the concept of the 'Sophoclean hero', and on the dramatic structure of the plays. Seven studies of the individual plays make up the book, drawn together by a brief concluding chapter.

The Plays of Sophocles aims to help readers to understand why Sophocles is still worth reading, or going to see in the theatre, in the twenty-first century, and to show how far Sophoclean scholarship has moved in recent decades from the once prevalent view that he was a pious religious conformist who had nothing very profound or original to say, but who said it very beautifully.

The Plays of Euripides

James Morwood

ISBN 1 85399 614 9

No book on all the plays of Euripides has been published since 1967. In the meantime there has been a revolution in the way we view not only classical drama generally, but this particular dramatist.

As well as reflecting this revolution, *The Plays of Euripides* seeks to show that the playwright was constantly reinventing himself. A truly Protean figure, he set out on a new journey in each of the nineteen plays. Short essays on all of them are rounded off by an epilogue which identifies some underlying themes but continues to insist on the diversity of this great dramatist.

The Greek and Roman Historians

Timothy E. Duff

ISBN 1 85399 601 7

What did 'history' mean to the Greeks and Romans? What were the aims of the ancient historians and how did they evaluate their sources? This volume traces the development of conceptions of history and its practice from Homer to the writers of the Roman Empire. It serves as an introduction to the great historians of the ancient world and contains sections on Herodotos, Thucydides, Xenophon, Polybios, Sallust, Livy, Velleius, Tacitus, Suetonius, Plutarch, Arrian and Dio, as well as on some other historians whose work now survives only in fragments.

Brief analyses of the events which form the background to each historian's work set the writers in their historical context. Each section is self-contained and may be read on its own; but specific attention is paid to links between the different historians, and the ways in which they were influenced by or competed with one another.